The Promise of
HEAVEN

DISCOVERING OUR
ETERNAL
HOME

DOUGLAS
CONNELLY

InterVarsity Press
Downers Grove, Illinois

InterVarsity Press
P.O. Box 1400, Downers Grove, IL 60515
World Wide Web: www.ivpress.com
E-mail: mail@ivpress.com

InterVarsity Press® is the book-publishing division of InterVarsity Christian Fellowship/USA®, a student movement active on campus at hundreds of universities, colleges and schools of nursing in the United States of America, and a member movement of the International Fellowship of Evangelical Students. For information about local and regional activities, write Public Relations Dept., InterVarsity Christian Fellowship/USA, 6400 Schroeder Rd., P.O. Box 7895, Madison, WI 53707-7895.

All Scripture quotations, unless otherwise indicated, are taken from the Holy Bible, New International Version® NIV®. *Copyright ©1973, 1978, 1984 by International Bible Society. Used by permission of Zondervan Publishing House. All rights reserved.*

Cover photograph: Mark A. Johnson/The Stock Market

ISBN 0-8308-2231-3

Printed in the United States of America ∞

Library of Congress Cataloging-in-Publication Data

Connelly, Douglas, 1949-
　The promise of heaven : discovering our eternal home / Douglas Connelly.
　　p. cm.
　Includes bibliographical references.
　ISBN 0-8308-2231-3 (cloth : alk. paper)
　1. Heaven—Christianity. I. Title.

BT846.2.C56 2000
236'.24—dc21

00-039581

15	14	13	12	11	10	9	8	7	6	5	4	3	2	1
11	10	09	08	07	06	05	04	03	02	01	00			

To Bill and LaVelle Hamrick,
two gracious Christians who helped us
when we needed it most
and who became treasured friends

Contents

A Word of Thanks

Karen (my wife), Kyle, Kevin, Kim and Mike (my children), and Paul and Mary (my parents) are a constant source of encouragement, love and grace to me. My Cross Church family holds me up in their hearts and their prayers. Cindy Bunch-Hotaling and all the people at InterVarsity Press do a great job of shepherding my books to readers. Granddaughter Allison makes me realize the importance of investing ourselves in the lives of those we love. Friends like Bill and LaVelle Hamrick help me sense what it will be like to have joyful fellowship together in heaven forever.

1

Preparing a Place

"Heaven is a prepared place
for prepared people."

BUMPER STICKER

My friend was dying. Her breaths came as ragged gasps. I didn't talk because I didn't want her to try to hold up her end of the conversation. In a whisper she said, "Do me (gasp) a favor (gasp) please." "Anything," I naively answered. "Sing," she wheezed. "Here, in your hospital room?" I asked. She nodded. "What do you want me to sing?" It took a few heavy breaths for her to get enough strength, but I finally heard, "'In the Garden'—my favorite."

So I sang. Nurses looked in with wonder. Hospital guests

stared in disbelief. One patient walking in the hallway moved just to the edge of the door to listen. The words floated over my friend's heart like a quieting stream.

"I think I saw heaven last night," she whispered. "I saw the lights of a great city—and it looked like home."

Probably no word brings more peace and calm into our lives than the word *heaven*. When we are doing what is most enjoyable, whether it's sitting on the porch of a mountain lodge watching a sunset or curling up by a cozy fire on a cold night or dozing in a hammock on a warm summer afternoon, we find ourselves saying, "This is heaven." Secure, happy experiences give us glimpses of what heaven must be like.

Thoughts of heaven help us make it through difficult times too. When we stand at the casket of someone we love, we hold on to the hope that we will embrace that person again some day. When the pressures of life seem insurmountable or when the pain seems unbearable, our hearts hunger for the refuge of heaven. No thought brings more comfort to parents of a Down syndrome child or more assurance to an older person struggling with the onset of Alzheimer's disease than the hope of future wholeness in heaven.

But heaven is a lot more than an enjoyable experience or a pleasurable dream. Heaven is a place, a real place, a place none of us has ever been but a place we can't wait to see. Heaven is God's home. It's the center of all that's good and pure and right. Sometimes it seems that this world of disappointment and pain and sorrow is the only reality we will ever know. But in our hearts we sense that there is a better place. Beyond this life another world exists, a world we can only begin to imagine, a place called heaven.

Looking for Answers

My interest in heaven began that day in my friend's hospital room. I had heard about heaven, of course, and thought about it a little. But now I wanted to know more. What is heaven like — and why does it seem like home to a person who is so near to death? If our happiest, most peace-filled moments are a reflection of heaven, if heaven is a refuge from the pain and suffering that mark this life, I wanted to find out as much as I could about it.

Maybe that is why you are reading this book. You've heard about heaven and even had some ideas about it, but now you want more. You want information, but you are also looking for assurance about your own future in heaven. You want to know what to expect when you get to heaven — who you will see and what you will do. Maybe you aren't particularly anxious to see heaven for a while, but you *are* interested in learning how to live right now in anticipation of heaven.

> "It's especially interesting to us earthbound people
> that our place in Heaven's High-Rise is already prepared,
> and since it's part of our inheritance,
> it comes at no cost to us." —DON BAKER

Whatever your interest in heaven, I want to welcome you on this journey with me. We'll learn some fascinating things, but we will also be challenged to change some things in our lives here and now. The truth of heaven is not just a wish for the good life someday. What we discover will call us to live a great life today.

It's not hard to find information about heaven. Local bookstores have several books on the subject. Internet sites about heaven abound. Lots of people claim to have visited heaven or been taken on a tour of heaven—and their stories captivate large audiences. Information about heaven is not the problem. What's hard to find is *reliable* information about heaven. Most of us can imagine what we would like heaven to be. We might be impressed with the experiences of people who claim to have seen heaven. We might search the religious traditions of the world, seeking insight in the life beyond. But what we really need is the *truth* about heaven. If I'm standing beside the hospital bed of someone I love who is dying or if I am facing life's final valley myself, someone else's experience or speculation about heaven won't help much. What will bring comfort and peace is the truth about what lies beyond death's door.

The only reliable source of information about what happens after death is the Bible, God's Word. We can trust what the Bible says because only one person has passed through death, conquered it forever and come back to tell us about it. That person was Jesus Christ. Jesus put his stamp of approval on everything the Old Testament said and on everything his personal representatives would write in the New Testament. We can trust what the Bible says!

So this book will explore the Bible's teaching about heaven. The truth we discover together may not match up with what we imagine about heaven or what we've heard about heaven. Some of our most cherished beliefs may turn out to be inaccurate. But our goal is not just to get one more opinion on the subject. Our goal is to find out what God has to say about heaven and then to bring our viewpoint into line with his. It is when we begin to think biblically about heaven that we will find genuine comfort and strength in the face of death. We won't be looking for the next television special or best-selling book about a visit to heaven. We will be looking for a city built by God.

God's Map

The word *heaven* is used more than five hundred times in sixty different biblical books. Heaven in Scripture refers to one of three places. The atmosphere around the earth is called heaven. The "clouds of heaven" or "rain from heaven" or the "birds of heaven" populate the first level of heaven (Deuteronomy 11:11; Psalm 147:8 NASB; Daniel 7:13).[1] The second place called heaven in the Bible is the cosmic heaven—the heaven of the moon and sun and stars (Genesis 1:14-17; Deuteronomy 4:19 NASB). Most often the word refers to the "third heaven," the dwelling place of God.

The Bible always describes heaven as *up*. The apostle Paul tells us that when Jesus came to earth, he *descended* from heaven, and when he left earth, he *ascended* into heaven (Ephesians 4:8-10). The angels told the disciples who had seen Jesus leave the earth that Jesus had been taken *up* from them into heaven (Acts 1:11). When God searches for a faithful human being, he "looks *down* from heaven" (Psalm 53:2), and when human beings contemplate God, we look *up* (Psalm 121:1).

The Bible's portrayal of heaven as above us is, of course, a figure of speech. Heaven cannot be spotted through a telescope or by the cameras of an interplanetary space vehicle. Heaven is in another realm that human observation cannot see or sense. Heaven is a place on God's map, not on the astronomer's star charts.

But that doesn't mean that heaven is imaginary. It is a real place. Jesus told his disciples that he was going to prepare a *place* for them (John 14:2). Heaven is not a dream nor a fantasy. In fact, in contrast to earth and the universe around us, which are in the process of passing away, heaven is stable, permanent and eternal (Hebrews 11:8-10).

The Bible uses some fascinating images to picture what heaven will be like. The writers of Scripture mingled "the familiar and the unfamiliar, the earthly and the more than earthly"[2] to draw our attention to heaven's glory. Jesus spoke of heaven as a place for people to live—as a great house filled with many rooms or apartments (John 14:1-3). Sometimes heaven is pictured as a magnificent temple, ringing with the joyful worship of God's people (Revelation 4—5; Isaiah 6:1). The apostle John concluded the book of Revelation with a picture of heaven as a glorious city, complete with walls and gates and streets (Revelation 21—22). Heaven is also portrayed as a garden paradise (Revelation 22:1-2), a banquet hall (Luke 14:15-24; Revelation 19:1-9) and a sports arena where victors are crowned for their accomplishments (1 Corinthians 9:24-27). The image used most often of heaven in Scripture is the picture of a kingdom, ruled by a powerful king, the Lord God (Revelation 11:15; 12:10; 19:6).

Our Father's House
"Where is Grandma if she's not here anymore?" Our three-year-old was looking into a casket where his grandmother seemed to be sleeping. "Her body is here for a while," we tried to explain, "but

Grandma is in heaven with Jesus." When a believer in Christ dies, we say that he or she has gone to heaven. The person's spirit is with Christ in a place prepared for them by Jesus himself. "I am going," Jesus said, "to prepare a place for you" (John 14:2). That "place" Jesus called "my Father's house"—a place of glory and rest and blessing.

Jesus has been preparing his Father's house for two thousand years, and it is already teeming with activity. Three groups inhabit heaven today.

First, heaven is the dwelling place of the holy angels of God. When Jesus was born in Bethlehem, an angel announced his birth to shepherds, and suddenly the sky was filled with "a great company of the *heavenly* host" praising God (Luke 2:13, emphasis added). When the angels left the hillside, Luke says, they went "into heaven" (Luke 2:15). Jesus often spoke of the angels "in heaven" (Matthew 18:10; Mark 12:25; 13:32). When the apostle John saw heaven in a vision, millions of angels surrounded God's throne (Revelation 5:11). As the servants of God, angels minister here on earth to those who will inherit salvation (Hebrews 1:14), but they live in heaven.[3]

The second group inhabiting heaven right now are the spirits of Old Testament believers. Before Jesus died on the cross, Old Testament believers who died went to paradise or Sheol (Luke 16:22; 23:43). It was a place of rest and comfort, but it was not the immediate presence of God. When Jesus ascended into heaven after his resurrection, he took all the believers who were in paradise with him (Ephesians 4:8; Hebrews 11:39-40). Abraham, Moses, David and Ruth are now in the Father's house with Christ.

The third group in heaven consists of the spirits of New Testament believers, those who have lived and died since Christ's ascension. The apostle Paul states with absolute confidence that when we are absent from the body in death, we find ourselves at home with the Lord (2 Corinthians 5:8).

Believers who die, of course, join two others in heaven—Jesus Christ and God the Father. Jesus left heaven's glory and came to earth as a human being. But after his sacrifice on the cross and his resurrection from the dead, Jesus ascended back into heaven. When the early Christian Stephen was being stoned to death, he looked up to heaven and saw Jesus "standing at the right hand of God" (Acts 7:55-56). Jesus is in heaven today at the center of all that God is doing. But Jesus is not just sitting in heaven waiting to return to earth someday. His ministry focuses on us. The Bible says that Jesus prays for us and pleads our case before God the Father. Romans 8:34 says, "Christ Jesus, who died—more than that, who was raised to life—is at the right hand of God and is also interceding for us." In 1 John 2:1 we read this: "If anybody does sin, we have one who speaks to the Father in our defense—Jesus

Christ, the Righteous One." Jesus has pioneered the way into the presence of the Father (Hebrews 9:24). Because we have been made clean by his eternal sacrifice, we can come before God with absolute confidence. At the Father's side is our Savior (Hebrews 10:19-22).

We realize that heaven does not contain God the Father. God is pure spirit and is greater than his creation. But the Bible pictures heaven as the place where the Father displays his glorious presence. It's where God's throne is, the center of God's activity in the universe. The great Old Testament prophet Moses asks God to "look down from heaven, your holy dwelling place, and bless your people Israel" (Deuteronomy 26:15). When Jesus taught his disciples to pray, he addressed God as "our Father in *heaven*" (Matthew 6:9, emphasis added). When human beings are allowed to see heaven, they perceive God as brilliant light or a burning ember (Ezekiel 1:27; Revelation 4:3). Because God the Father is spirit, he has no body or parts. The Bible sometimes uses phrases like "the eyes of God" or "the arm of God" to picture his activity, but in reality God has no arm or eye. God the Holy Spirit is also pure spirit without a body. Only one member of the Trinity has a body, Jesus Christ. He became fully human at his conception; he was raised to life in a glorified body and he remains in that body today.

> "Simply put, we're going to be with a Person
> as much as we are going to live in a place.
> The presence of Christ
> is what makes heaven heaven." — JOHN MACARTHUR

I do not think we will "see" God the Father in heaven. We will see what John and Ezekiel saw — a figure of a person surrounded by brilliant light. The only person we will see is Jesus, but we will also see him as John saw him — the awesome, glorious God-man, the exalted Lord of all. We won't run up and shake hands with Jesus when we see him. John was Jesus' closest friend on earth, but when John saw the ascended Lord sixty years after Jesus had gone to heaven, John didn't slap Jesus on the back and say, "It's great to see you again." John fell on his face in adoration and worship (Revelation 1:12-17). In Christ all the fullness of God dwells in bodily form (Colossians 2:9). We will only see Jesus in heaven, but he will be enough.

Headed for Heaven?

According to one Gallup Poll,[4] 90 percent of Americans believe that heaven exists — and 77 percent give themselves excellent prospects of going there! In the same poll, 73 percent said they believe in hell, but only 6 percent think they will end up there. A religious magazine surveyed its readers and asked, "Why do you believe you will go to heaven?" The most popular answers were

☐ I have always tried to live a good life.

☐ I'm not as bad as other people.

☐ I have tried to be kind to everyone.

I've encountered some of the most bizarre ideas about heaven from other people. You've heard some too. Saint Peter, for example, will not be standing at heaven's gates to ask questions of those who enter. That idea comes from twisting what Jesus said to Peter in Matthew 16:17-19. Jesus told Peter that he would give him the keys of the kingdom—meaning Peter (and the other apostles) would play a crucial role in God's new program, the Christian church. Jesus also said that the gates of *hell* would never overpower Christ's program or Christ's people. Nothing is said, however, about Peter unlocking heaven's gates for those who want to come in.

The American humorist Mark Twain thought heaven would be incredibly boring—sitting on clouds, strumming harps, singing the same song over and over. A lot of people think of heaven as perpetual retirement with nothing to do. But that is *not* the picture the Bible paints. Rest? Yes. Retirement? Never!

"The sobering news about Heaven, however,
is that many of the 'roads to Heaven' people take
will never get them there."—DON BAKER

Probably the most widely held myth about heaven is that people who go there (especially babies) get their "wings" and become angels. That is simply not true. Human beings never become angelic beings—and we shouldn't want to! Redeemed human beings will have a glory far greater than angels in God's eternity.

Living Now in Light of the Not Yet

God has given us wonderful insights in his Word about heaven. He doesn't want us in the dark or in a fog about our eternal destiny. He hasn't told us about heaven to make us complacent but to encourage us to greater faithfulness—faithfulness demonstrated in believers like George Strickland.

You had to be careful when you hugged Mr. Strickland. He was so thin and small you were afraid he would break. But when Mr. Strickland got up to speak in a meeting, a hush fell over everyone. His words were always worth listening to. He was a man who had spent long years serving and walking with the Lord.

One Sunday evening an usher handed me a note that Mr. Strickland had been taken to the hospital that afternoon. As the service closed, I left the church and went to his bedside. He seemed asleep, but when I spoke his name, his eyes opened. He said, "What are *you* doing here?" I replied, "What are you doing here?" In a quiet voice he said, "I won't be here much longer. This afternoon I had a dream about going to heaven. I believe the Lord will take me home soon." Within twenty-four hours Mr. Strickland was dead.

At George Strickland's funeral I said with absolute confidence that I believed our friend was with the Lord. I didn't say it because Mr. Strickland had tried to live a good life or because he wasn't as bad as other people. I didn't say it because he was a church member for sixty years. I didn't even say it because he had dreamed about going to heaven. I made that statement because many years earlier George Strickland had bowed his heart in faith to Jesus Christ. Because of God's grace, when this dear man closed his eyes on all that surrounded him on earth, he opened them in the Father's house in the presence of his Savior and Lord.

2

The Final Frontier

*" 'Some day you will read in the papers that Moody is dead.
Don't you believe a word of it!
At that moment I shall be more alive than I am right now.' . . .
Four months after speaking these words,
the great evangelist Dwight Moody, was with the Lord."*

JOHN POLLOCK

I celebrated my fiftieth birthday this year—and became a grandpa! Both events made me realize how short life really is. When we think about the wonder of heaven, we are also faced with the fact that heaven lies beyond a terrifying experience called death.

Our culture doesn't like to face death. We do all we can to insulate ourselves from it. We don't like to see death or smell it or touch it. Elderly people and terminally ill people used to die at home, surrounded by those who loved them. Now we have institutions where we can put people who are dying. If the advocates of physician-assisted suicide have their way, we may soon have institutions that speed up the process of death. The response of our society to death has been to ignore it, to cover it up, to try and outdistance it. You might even be tempted to skip this chapter and move on to something less painful.

The problem with ignoring or denying death is that when death finally comes, we aren't ready to face it. We aren't prepared for what death brings. The very thing we hoped would never happen to us is suddenly happening. By refusing to face death's reality, we keep ourselves in ignorance about it. If you ask a doctor about death, she can tell you what happens biologically when you die, but medical science can't explain what it feels like to die. Basic questions still persist: Do we live on after death? Are we awake? Are we in heaven—or hell? Philosophers have discussed the questions surrounding death for centuries. They can tell us what they *think* will happen, but that's all.

Scientific investigation can't answer our questions. Human reason and speculation don't help us. What we need is the testimony of someone who has gone through death and then come back to life to tell us what to expect. In the Bible a few people die and come back to life, but they never say anything about their experience. Dozens of people in our day have written books and gone on television talk shows to describe their "life-after-death" experiences. The problem is their experience may or may not be my experience.

Fortunately we do have the reliable testimony of one man who went through death and who was raised back to life. Through the writers of the New Testament, Jesus has told us what death is like and what we can expect after we die. The Bible doesn't come to us with long philosophical discussions about death. It's not just a book of wishful dreams either. It is God's Word, and it was written so we can say, "I *know* what lies beyond death. I don't know everything because God hasn't told us everything, but what God has said, I can trust."

Setting Sail

The New Testament writers used several metaphors or word pictures to describe what death will be like for the Christian. Each image is designed to bring assurance and peace to our hearts as we face the deaths of people we love and as we think about our own death. If the thought of death brings terror to your heart, begin to replace those fearful images with God's view of what death is like.

The Bible most often pictures death as *sleep* (2 Chronicles 9:31; Psalm 13:3; Daniel 12:2; John 11:11-13; 1 Corinthians 11:30; 15:51). Sleep, like death, is a temporary experience and ends in a great awakening. I think the image of sleep is used for death so often in Scripture because sleep and death are both universal experiences. From infancy to old age, human beings need sleep. When

I've worked hard, I look forward to lying down in a refreshing sleep. I don't fear sleep or try to avoid it; I embrace it. We close our eyes in anticipation of a new day. For the Christian, death is falling asleep to all we have known in this realm and waking up in Christ's presence.

Death is also compared to *taking down a tent*. Our present bodies are our temporary dwelling places. The apostle Paul calls the body "the earthly tent we live in" (2 Corinthians 5:1). He adds later, "While we are in this tent, we groan and are burdened" (2 Corinthians 5:4). Our bodies get tired and sick; we experience pain and paralysis. But the assurance of the Christian is that when this earthly tent is destroyed, "we have a building from God, an eternal house in heaven, not built by human hands" (2 Corinthians 5:1). Death is the first step in a wonderful process that will eventually bring us a permanent, glorified body that will never age or decay or require a wheelchair.

In his letter to the Christians in the city of Philippi, Paul used another image to describe death. He pictured death as a *departure*.

> If I am to go on living in the body, this will mean fruitful labor for me. Yet what shall I choose? I do not know! I am torn between the two: I desire to depart and be with Christ, which is better by far; but it is more necessary for you that I remain in the body. (Philippians 1:22-24)

The word *depart* was used of a ship that had been loosened from its moorings and had set sail for a new destination. The "mooring" holding Paul to this earthly realm was his dedication to the work God had given him. But tugging at his heart was a deep desire to pull up anchor, untie the ropes and sail away. Paul's departure at death would not be to some unknown destination. He would depart and be with Christ. The phrase Paul uses implies a conscious, intimate, face-to-face fellowship with Christ. Paul wasn't going to sleep in death. His body would sleep, but he would be with Christ.

Probably the most comforting New Testament image of death is that of *coming home.* In most people's minds, home represents a place of security and rest and acceptance. The biblical writers looked at heaven that way. Paul in 2 Corinthians 5:6-8 describes two places the Christian can call home. First, we can be at home "in the body," that is, in our present realm. While we are at home here, however, we are "away from the Lord." As much as Paul loved life and the people he ministered to, he longed to be in the second place called home: "[I] would prefer to be away from the body and at home with the Lord." When we are absent from the body, when our spirit separates from our body in death, we find ourselves "at home" with the Lord.

"[Our friend] Gertrude died about ten minutes ago.
I wonder what thrilling experiences she's having
at this very moment."—PETER MARSHALL

Clinging to God's Promises

As wonderful and assuring as the biblical images of death are, they are backed up by something even more secure—the solid promises of God. Those who have never believed in Christ may shudder at the prospect of dying, but we who are in Christ have the anchor of God's Word holding us secure.

For the Christian, death is no longer feared. In our human weakness we still look at death as an ominous foe, but God has given us a specific promise that whatever death brings, it will not separate us from him. In the book of Romans the apostle Paul makes a list of all the things that we think might separate us from God. The very first item on his list is death: "For I am convinced that neither *death* nor life, neither angels nor demons, neither the present nor the future, nor any powers, neither height nor depth, nor anything else in all creation, will be able to separate us from the love of God that is in Christ Jesus our Lord" (Romans 8:38-39, emphasis added).

If you are afraid of death, get a grip on that promise. Nothing will be able to separate you from God and his love—not even death! God won't lose you; he won't forget you; he won't abandon you in death. God confirms his promise in Hebrews 13:5 when he says, "Never will I leave you; never will I forsake you." The writer of Hebrews then tells us how to respond to God's promise: "So we say with confidence, 'The Lord is my helper; I will not be afraid' " (Hebrews 13:6).

Along with the fear of death, God promises to remove the sting of death. Paul almost shouts in 1 Corinthians 15:55, "Where, O death, is your victory? Where, O death, is your sting?" The ability of death to inflict permanent pain was removed by Jesus' victory over death. It can't terrorize us anymore. Death for us is falling asleep in Jesus; it's setting sail to a place called home.

I walked into a hospital room a few years ago to see a woman who was dying. I was told that she was in a coma and was near death, but she seemed so uneasy. She moved her head from side to side, and her arms and legs shifted uncomfortably. Soft moans and cries drifted over the room. A nurse who was the woman's friend came into the room, and we talked quietly about the woman's unease. We sensed that our friend was not fearful of death but was probably concerned about her husband, who would be left to care for himself. Her husband, who was almost blind, had depended on his wife for years. We assured her that other Christians would take care of her husband. We reminded her of friends living nearby who would see that her husband had groceries and a ride to the doctor's office. As we talked, the woman quieted and a calm came over her. We told her that she could let go of this life and go to be with Christ. After a brief prayer, we left—and within an hour she had died. For her the "sting of death" was the responsibility she was leaving behind. But even that need was met by faithful believers who stepped in to care for an ailing husband.

> "Death will some day be destroyed,
> but it is still a most painful experience
> which all of us must face."—JOSEPH BAYLY

Death is also robbed of its uncertainty for a Christian. Jesus has walked the dark valley ahead of us, beaming the bright light of truth along the path. We can face death knowing that this final enemy is a defeated enemy.

The promises God gives to his children are not just dry declarations to be repeated over and over at the time of death. His Word is not just ink on paper. Along with the clear promises we read in the Bible, we also have the inner witness of the Holy Spirit who brings assurance to our hearts that what God declares in his Word is true. I hope as you read the passages of Scripture in this chapter, you sensed God's Spirit affirm their truth in your heart and mind. It's as if God puts his own declaration point, his own "amen," on what his Word says. Paul puts it this way: "The Spirit himself testifies with our spirit that we are God's children" (Romans 8:16). The apostle John was certain of the same truth: "You have an anointing from the Holy One, and all of you know the truth" (1 John 2:20).

I need to add that God's promises are only for those who claim Jesus Christ as their Savior. If you don't know Christ, if you have never personally trusted in him, you *ought* to be terrified of death.

You will face death alone, and you will face eternity separated from Christ. But the good news is you don't have to live in fear of death. God offers you eternal life today if you, in faith, receive Christ as your Savior. He died on the cross for you; he rose again in victory for you. He will change you and cleanse you from sin at this moment if you will accept his grace and forgiveness.

Living Now in Light of the Not Yet

I often find myself in hospital rooms and living rooms as families watch a loved one die. Sometimes they sit in silence. Sometimes they speak or whisper expressions of love into the dying person's ear. The tenderest scenes I have witnessed at a deathbed are loving spouses or children reminding a believing wife, mother or father of God's promises to those who are his own children. Often the words of Scripture are the last words we whisper to loved ones who lie in the darkness of death waiting for the daybreak of heaven.

We are tempted at times to wish a believer back who has gone to be with Christ. The pain of separation can be crushing. The Bible, however, says that to be with the Lord is "better by far" than anything we can know or experience here (Philippians 1:23). We miss those who have died, but they are in a place that is not just better, but better by far.

Elizabeth Elliot, an author and former missionary, tells about a time when she and her native guide were following a footpath through the South American jungle. The trail ended at a deep ravine. The only way across was a fallen tree. The guide jumped on the tree and started across. Elizabeth Elliot stood frozen by fear. When her guide saw her hesitation, he came back, grasped her hand and led her safely to the other side.[1]

At the deep ravine of death, we all hesitate. The final enemy has been conquered, but it is still an enemy. Then Jesus, the one who already tasted death for us, takes us by the hand and leads us safely to the other side. Because he has come through death as a victor, Jesus gives us confidence and calm as we face our own final frontier.

3

Glimpses of Glory

*"God whispers to us in health and prosperity, but, being hard of hearing,
we fail to hear God's voice. Whereupon God turns up the amplifier
by means of suffering. Then his voice booms."*

C. S. LEWIS

*I*t *might surprise you to know* that several people in the Bible actually saw heaven—and lived to tell about it! These weren't the after-death experiences that grab headlines today. These were *pre-death* visions of what heaven is like. A few people got to see heaven before they died as an encouragement for the rest of us.

The early Christian leader Stephen gave a courageous defense of Jesus in front of an increasingly hostile crowd. At the end of his speech, Stephen "looked up to heaven and saw the glory of God, and Jesus standing at the right hand of God" (Acts 7:55). The crowd never considered the possibility that Stephen was telling the truth. In the blindness of their hatred, they stoned him to death.

The apostle Paul was taken to heaven in a vision. He calls what he saw "paradise"—a garden of beauty and peace. He was told things that human language could never fully express. That's about all we know about Paul's vision because God specifically prohibited Paul from telling any more (2 Corinthians 12:1-6). Paul's vision was not to be used for self-glory or to promote his latest book. In fact, God balanced the glory of that vision with a painful "thorn" in Paul's body as a constant reminder of Paul's absolute dependence on the Lord (2 Corinthians 12:7-10).

By far the most sustained vision of heaven came to the apostle John as he wrote the book of Revelation. Almost the entire book is written from the vantage point of heaven. After John saw Jesus in his majesty (Revelation 1) and heard Jesus speak to each of the seven churches to which the book was addressed (Revelation 2—3), John was told, "Come up here [into heaven], and I will show you what must take place after this" (Revelation 4:1). The rest of the book is written as if John were standing on the edge of heaven. He first watches events unfold in heaven (such as mighty angels carrying seven bowls of God's wrath), and then he turns and see how those events affect the inhabitants of earth (the judgments that come on the earth as each bowl is poured out).

When We All Get to Heaven

Within the long visual tapestry of the book of Revelation, John records three scenes in heaven that give us deeper insight into what it will be like for us to be in heaven. The first detailed scene is in Revelation 4 and 5—an incredible scene of worship and praise to God that we will examine later in chapter six.

> "Oh, Christian brethren, what is our light affliction
> when compared to such an eternity as this?
> Shame on us if we murmur and complain and turn back,
> with such a heaven before our eyes!"—J. C. RYLE

The second detailed scene of heaven in the book of Revelation is not very long, but we learn some very significant facts from what John says. In this section of Revelation, Jesus is opening a sealed scroll one wax seal at a time. As each seal is broken, a new scene leaps before John's eyes.

When he opened the fifth seal, I saw under the altar the souls of those who had been slain because of the word of God and the testimony they had maintained. They called out in a loud voice, "How long, Sovereign Lord, holy and true, until you judge the inhabitants of the earth and avenge our blood?" Then each of them was given a white robe, and they were told to wait a little longer, until the number of their fellow servants and brothers who were to be killed as they had been was completed." (Revelation 6:9-11)

As the fifth seal on the scroll is broken, John sees the souls (or spirits) of men and women who have died. They had been violently killed "because of the word of God and the testimony they had maintained" (Revelation 6:9). These people have not yet experienced the resurrection of their bodies. John sees them as "souls"; their bodies have not been glorified yet.

This scene parallels the experience of Christians who die today. Our bodies remain on earth, but our spirits go to be with the Lord in heaven. We don't simply float around, however, as ghostlike spirits. These "souls" in heaven obviously function within temporary bodies of some kind. They are clothed in white robes, and they are able to speak in loud voices to God.

What these martyrs say seems shocking. They plead with God to judge the inhabitants of the earth and avenge their blood. We have believed that once we get to heaven, we won't know what is happening on earth. How can heaven be a place of joy if we are able to see the wars and cruelty and injustice on earth? But these believers had at least *some* knowledge of events on earth. They knew that God's vengeance had not yet been carried out on the people responsible for their deaths. God even told them about some of the bad things that would happen on earth. He informed these martyrs that even more followers of Christ would have to die before the fullness of his judgment would be carried out.

This passage has changed how I think about heaven! After we die, we may have limited knowledge of what is happening on earth. That knowledge seems to center on the progress of the fulfillment of God's plan for human history. We will see God working out exactly what he has purposed to do. Heaven *will* mean the end of tears and sorrow but not until God has brought everything in his plan to completion. One other fact we need to keep in mind is that we will see all that God is doing with a new perspective. We will look through redeemed eyes as God brings human history to its final collapse.

We've also been mistaken in our assumption that we won't remember what happened to us during our life on earth. These martyrs certainly remembered the suffering they had experienced for their identification with Christ. They remembered that they had been violently and unjustly killed for their testimony. The deeds we do on earth will not be forgotten but will "follow" us to heaven (Revelation 14:13). Our rewards and positions of responsibility in heaven will be the direct indication of the faithfulness of our lives on earth. We won't forget our "righteous acts"; we will be clothed in a brilliant garment that represents those acts of goodness and obedience to Christ (Revelation 19:7-8). The Bible makes a direct connection between our lives on earth and our future lives in heaven.

Present Trials — Future Glory

John's third detailed observation of heaven is in Revelation 7. The first thing John sees is an enormous gathering of people—men and women from every ethnic, racial and language group on earth. This multitude joins with the other inhabitants of heaven in shouting praise and honor to God and to Jesus, the Lamb of God. Then John is told who these people are.

> These are they who have come out of the great tribulation; they have washed their robes and made them white in the blood of the Lamb. (Revelation 7:14)

It is obvious that the people John sees are genuine believers in Jesus Christ. They know what it means to be washed from sin's penalty by trusting in Jesus. These people also know what it is like to suffer. They "have come out of the great tribulation." At the end of this age in God's program, the world will experience a time of judgment from God unlike anything ever experienced before. As that time of great tribulation unfolds, the followers of Christ will become the targets of persecution and attack worldwide. On one hand these martyrs for the faith will cry out to God to bring vengeance on those who were responsible for their slaughter (as we saw in Revelation 6). But on the other hand they will experience the joy and peace of heaven as a relief from their suffering on earth. They have passed through the trial of their faith into heaven's glory.

I am impressed that these believers who stand and worship in God's presence are given something to do in heaven.

> They are before the throne of God
>   and *serve him* day and night in his temple.
>   (Revelation 7:15, emphasis added)

The service John describes parallels the service of priests in the Old Testament who supervised the worship in the temple in Jerusalem. This multitude will have individual responsibilities assigned to them, and they will carry out those responsibilities with joy. I hope you aren't under the impression that heaven will consist of sitting in a rocking chair on the front porch of a heavenly mansion. Heaven will be a place of incredible activity. We will know the satisfaction of serving God without fear of failure or rejection. Each of us will have tasks that will fully engage our abilities and our passion for accomplishment.

Heaven will also bring the security of being sheltered by God. John says that "he who sits on the throne will spread his tent over them" (Revelation 7:15). John's language points back again to the Old Testament and the shelter of the tabernacle, Israel's worship center. God spreads his protection over us.

In the shelter of God's care, his people also experience eternal satisfaction.

> Never again will they hunger;
>   never again will they thirst.
> The sun will not beat upon them,
>   nor any scorching heat. (Revelation 7:16)

The concerns that consume so much of our time and energy on earth will all be met in heaven. Providing food and shelter for ourselves and our families will be worries of the past. What we will experience instead is the direct provision of the Shepherd, Jesus himself.

> For the Lamb at the center of the
>   Throne will be their shepherd;
>   he will lead them to springs of living water.
> And God will wipe away every tear
>   from their eyes. (Revelation 7:17)

Heaven sets us free from all the things that burden our minds here on earth. My concern for my wife as she leaves for work in the morning or my prayer for our son's protection as he walks through the school doors will be unnecessary. The struggle to pay each month's bills and to provide for my family's needs will be gone. Tears of sorrow or remorse or pain or loss are a regular part of life now but never in heaven.

Living Now in Light of the Not Yet

I'm fascinated by the fact that the explanation of heaven's joys was given to John by one of the elders around God's throne. This wasn't an angel's perspective or even God's personal declaration. These words came from someone who had experienced heaven personally as a redeemed human being. The elder knew what it was like to be sheltered under the protective tent of God. He knew the fulfillment of serving God as a priest. He had come to the springs of living water and been deeply satisfied. He knew what it was like to have God "wipe away every tear."

I think this phrase means far more than that we will never cry again. I think it means that in heaven we will come to understand *why* we cried so many tears here on earth. We will see the pattern of our lives from God's perspective, and we will see that everything God did was very good. We will finally see how God was working all things together for our good and for his glory. Right now our understanding of what God is doing is limited and even distorted by our own selfishness. We don't begin to comprehend why God would allow sickness to strike us or a crippling disease to afflict someone we love. We cry stinging tears over a child who seems to be far from the Lord, but we can't see what God is doing in that child's life to bring him or her back to him. But someday we will see the design that God is weaving, and even the tears we've cried here will be tenderly wiped away.

"When we've been there ten thousand years,
Bright shining as the sun,
We've no less days to sing God's praise,
Than when we first begun."
—JOHN NEWTON, "Amazing Grace"

A friend of mine carries a piece of a jigsaw puzzle around in his pocket. The picture is worn off and the edges are frayed, but he carries it as a constant reminder of how God works in his life. At a particularly difficult time in my friend's life, when he struggled with an out-of-control child and a collapsing business, his wife suggested that they put a jigsaw puzzle together over a holiday weekend. As they worked on the puzzle, they had the opportunity to talk about the issues that pressed so heavily on their hearts. When the puzzle was finished and the picture emerged, the wife pulled one piece from the center of the puzzle. "This piece is all you see of the puzzle of your life today," she said. "Only God sees the finished picture." The worn-out puzzle piece in his pocket is a constant reminder that God is working in his life, even when he cannot see how all the pieces fit together.

God knows what you are struggling with right now. If you are his child, that pain or loss is just one piece in God's plan—and it may be the piece that becomes the focal point of the finished design. God does not promise to explain our trials. He just asks us to trust him, to believe that he really is in control and that he has not abandoned us. But someday the picture he is putting together will be revealed in all its complexity and beauty. When that happens, the joy we will experience in the goodness of God will wipe out all the pain we feel right now.

When I think I'm having a bad day, I think about Jody Bowling. Jody has struggled with rheumatoid arthritis and its many complications for more than twenty years. She has had multiple surgeries and faces incredible pain every minute. Whenever she goes to the hospital (and it's often for weeks at a time), she takes a framed Bible verse that sits next to her bed. "I consider that our present sufferings are not worth comparing with the glory that will be revealed in us" (Romans 8:18). The puzzle piece of Jody's suffering has interlocked its beauty into many lives, including mine—and someday God will replace that suffering with overwhelming glory.

$$\underset{4}{\sdiagup | \diagdown}$$

We Shall Behold Him

"But . . . until [Jesus] comes, what?
Remember the watchwords: occupy, purify, watch and worship.
If you're engaged in those four things,
you won't have to get ready, you'll be ready!
No need to set a date or quit your job or dress in white.
Just live every day as if this were the one."

—CHUCK SWINDOLL

*M**ost of us think of heaven* as a place we go after we die. But one generation of Christians won't have to go through the dark valley of death. When Jesus returns, they will be changed forever.

A few years ago I got a call from a man who told me that he was selling something everyone needed. He was prepared to give me a great deal on cemetery lots! I was not in the best mood for a sales pitch, so I said, "Well, you may *think* everybody needs a cemetery lot, but I'm hoping I never need one."

That was followed by a long silence on the other end of the phone line. Finally he said, "Can you tell me why you won't need one?"

"To be honest with you," I said, "I'm hoping Jesus returns before I die."

I've never had a salesperson hang up so quickly.

One of the events we Christians eagerly wait for is the coming of Christ to claim us as his own. Those of us who are alive when Jesus returns will not experience death (no cemetery lots required). Instead we will be instantly clothed with glorified, eternal bodies. I certainly prefer that option to death. But what if Christ doesn't return before I die, and my body does end up in a cemetery somewhere? And what about all those Christians who have died in the last two thousand years?

The New You

We have already concluded from our study of the Bible that when a believer in Jesus Christ dies, that person's spirit immediately is in the presence of Christ. To be absent from the body is to find ourselves consciously present with the Lord (2 Corinthians 5:8). Our spirits remain in heaven until a great transformation takes place—the resurrection of our bodies.

God created human beings with a physical, visible dimension (the body) and with a spiritual, invisible dimension (the spirit).

Our spirits have already been changed. We have been made new in Christ. We are not waiting to be made new creatures; we *are* new creatures in Christ (2 Corinthians 5:17). The "old" person has been crucified with Christ, and a "new" person has been created by God's power. We don't *get* eternal life after we die; we *have* eternal life right now (John 3:16; 5:24; 1 John 5:11-12). Our bodies, however, are still subject to the old order of things. Our outward being is steadily decaying, but our inward being is constantly being renewed (2 Corinthians 4:16).

We sometimes think that our redemption as children of God will be complete when our spirits are carried into the presence of Christ at death. We think the ultimate end is simply to "go to heaven" after we die, but that's not the end. What began when we believed in Christ and were born again will only be complete and final when our bodies are resurrected and glorified. The body of death we live in now will give way to a resurrection body that will not age or decay. We will spend eternity as complete human beings—body and spirit (Romans 8:11-12; 2 Corinthians 4:14).

> "The Master himself will give the command.
> Archangel thunder! God's trumpet blast!
> He'll come down from heaven and the dead in Christ will rise."
> —1 THESSALONIANS 4:16, The Message

The person who pioneered the way to the resurrection is Jesus

Christ. Several people in biblical history were raised from the dead. Unfortunately all those people were raised in the same kind of bodies they had before to the same kind of life they had before—and they all died a second time! But Jesus was raised to a whole new kind of life. His body was transformed, changed, glorified. He would *never* die again. That had never happened before. We can almost hear the apostle Paul shout his affirmation of Jesus' resurrection in Romans 6: "For we know that since Christ was raised from the dead, he cannot die again; death no longer has mastery over him. The death he died, he died to sin once for all; but the life he lives, he lives to God" (Romans 6:9-10).

The good news for us in all of this is that because Jesus lives, we will also live (John 14:19). The One who brought Jesus up from the dead in resurrection glory will also give resurrection life to our bodies. In his spirit Jesus spent three days in paradise before his spirit and body were reunited (Matthew 12:40; Luke 23:43). Our spirits may spend centuries in heaven, and our bodies may crumble into dust, but the day will come when the voice of Christ will call those bodies back to life. God will change those bodies, and our spirits will inhabit glorified bodies forever.

What Kind of Body Would You Like?

Research scientists are searching feverishly for some way to slow or halt or even reverse the aging process. Every new insight or genetic theory is given frontline coverage in the news media. But nothing we can even imagine comes close to the wonder of our future bodies of glory. The Bible doesn't answer every question we have, but it gives us enough information to make us look forward with eager anticipation to our future transformation.

We can learn about our resurrection bodies first by examining what the Bible tells us about Jesus' resurrection body. The apostle John writes this: "Dear friends, now we are children of God, and what we will be has not yet been made known. But we know that when he appears, we shall be like him, for we shall see him as he is" (1 John 3:2). When Jesus appears we will be changed to be *like him.* Paul adds in Philippians 3:21 that Christ "will transform our lowly bodies so that they will be like his glorious body." We are being transformed right now in our *spirits* into the image of Christ (2 Corinthians 3:18); someday our *bodies* will be made like his too.

Another source we can access to learn more about our future bodies is a remarkable passage of Scripture. First Corinthians 15 contains a detailed explanation of the transformation that will take place in the future. After defending the absolute necessity of the resurrection of Jesus and the guaranteed certainty of our resurrection, Paul launches into a description of the similarities and contrasts between our present bodies and our future bodies.

The resurrection body will be connected to the present body

like a seed is connected to a new plant. "When you sow, you do not plant the body that will be, but just a seed, perhaps of wheat or of something else. But God gives it a body as he has determined, and to each kind of seed he gives its own body" (1 Corinthians 15:37-38).

When you plant a seed in the ground, the seed dies, but a new life, a new body, emerges. The new body is different from the seed in some ways, but in some ways it is the same. When he rose from the dead, Jesus looked essentially the same as he did before his death. But Jesus' body also had some new abilities—he could enter a room without opening the door, for example (John 20:19). Yet Jesus' body had substance. He could be touched; he could eat food (Luke 24:39, 42-43; 1 John 1:1). So there was continuity between Jesus' first body and his resurrection body.

The same will be true in our resurrection. I think we will look essentially the same as we do in this life. But there will also be some changes. We can't begin to comprehend those changes any more than we can envision a fully grown cornstalk by looking at a kernel of dried corn. I am convinced that the effects of sin's curse will be removed—no eyeglasses or wheelchairs or respirators will be needed. I *hope* that I will have more hair and less waistline in heaven. But we will be able to function just like Jesus functioned as a resurrected human being. We will eat at the great marriage supper with Abraham, Isaac and Jacob (Matthew 8:11), and we will drink wine with Jesus in commemoration of his death for our redemption (Matthew 26:29). But all the things that plague our bodies now will be gone forever.

The most intriguing part of Paul's declaration about our future bodies is the series of contrasts he draws between what we experience now and what we will experience then. Our present bodies, for example, are perishable, but our resurrection bodies will be imperishable. We won't deteriorate or grow old. Our present bodies are marked by dishonor; we bear the scars of sin and of a sinful world. Our new bodies will be bodies of glory and radiance. If that isn't enough, our present body is characterized by weakness, but our future body will be characterized by power. Today we get tired and sick; in the resurrection we will experience dynamic, self-sustaining energy.

I like Paul's final contrast best:

The first man Adam became a living being; the last Adam, a life-giving spirit. . . . The first man was of the dust of the earth, the second man from heaven. As was the earthly man, so are those who are of earth; and as is the man from heaven, so also are those who are of heaven. And just as we have borne the likeness of the earthly man, so shall we bear the likeness of the man from heaven. (1 Corinthians 15:45-49)

We look a lot like our father! Our present bodies bear the image of Adam, a noble being created in the image of God but fallen in sin and powerless to change his hopeless situation. Our resurrection bodies will bear the image of Jesus Christ, the Lord of glory.

Rapture Ahead!

God has even told us when this resurrection will take place. We will be changed at the rapture or the "catching away" of believers described in 1 Thessalonians 4. It's a passage that stirs a Christian's heart just to read:

> Brothers, we do not want you to be ignorant about those who fall asleep, or to grieve like the rest of men, who have no hope. We believe that Jesus died and rose again and so we believe that God will bring with Jesus those who have fallen asleep in him. According to the Lord's own word, we tell you that we who are still alive, who are left till the coming of the Lord, will certainly not precede those who have fallen asleep. For the Lord himself will come down from heaven, with a loud command, with the voice of the archangel and with the trumpet call of God, and the dead in Christ will rise first. After that, we who are still alive and are left will be caught up together with them in the clouds to meet the Lord in the air. And so we will be with the Lord forever. (1 Thessalonians 4:13-17)

Apparently some of the Thessalonian Christians were troubled by the fact that a few of the believers had died and Christ had not yet returned. What would happen to these brothers and sisters in

Christ? Would they miss the glory of Christ's return? Would they be left behind? Paul puts their minds at ease by explaining exactly what will happen when Christ returns for his people.

> "The degree to which we actually long for Christ's return is a
> measure of the spiritual condition of our lives at the moment.
> It also gives some measure of the degree to which few see the world
> as it really is, as God sees it, in bondage to sin and rebellion against God."
> —WAYNE GRUDEM

We don't have to grieve about those who have died in Christ. They won't be left out, and they won't be left behind. If the person who died was a believer in Jesus, the funeral and the grave are not the end. The rapture will bring a resurrection, and the resurrection will bring a reuniting of loved ones.

Paul then gives a great promise. He says that when Jesus returns, God will bring the spirits of those believers who have died back with Jesus. Those of us still alive when Christ returns will not have the priority in the rapture. We will not get a head start on those Christians who have died. The dead in Christ will rise first (1 Thessalonians 4:16). The bodies of all those who have died in Christ over the centuries will be reconstructed, resurrected to life and glorified—and then reunited with their spirits, which have been in the conscious presence of Christ since the moment of their deaths. Resurrected believers will be with Christ forever, no longer as spirits but as fully redeemed, complete human beings.

This is the future confidence of all those who have died in Christ. But what about those of us who are alive when Christ returns? What happens to us? Paul says that three supernatural events take place.

First, the Lord himself will come down from heaven (1 Thessalonians 4:16). I don't find any evidence that the return of Christ for his church will be a secret snatching away. The world will know that something is happening; they just won't know what. The Lord will descend with a shout—a military command. At the sound of his voice, every believer's body will awaken (John 5:25). Then the archangel will speak, a loud cry perhaps of triumph and praise. Angels couldn't keep silent at Jesus' birth when redemption's plan began; they will explode in praise again when redemption is completed. Finally will come a trumpet blast, a call to assembly.

We have already discussed the second supernatural act in this divine drama—the dead in Christ will be resurrected in glory (1 Thessalonians 4:17). The third supernatural event will be the transformation of believers who are still alive on earth when Christ returns. We will simply be changed and then caught up in the clouds to meet the Lord. The word translated "caught up" in 1 Thessalonians 4:17 means a sudden, forcible seizure. So we will be grabbed out of the world by an irresistible act of God. We will meet the Lord in the air as fully redeemed, glorified children of God, prepared to spend eternity in Christ's presence. We will be with those who have died in Christ, and we will remain with the Lord forever.

"When will [Jesus' final arrival] be?
Ah, my friend, I do not know.
No one knows its day or hour.
Therefore Jesus commands us to 'Watch. Stay awake.
Get ready. Prepare, prepare—and watch!' "
—WALTER WANGERIN

The entire drama of the rapture will take place in a moment of time: "Listen, I tell you a mystery: We will not all sleep, but we will all be changed—in a flash, in the twinkling of an eye, at the last trumpet. For the trumpet will sound, the dead will be raised imperishable, and we will be changed" (1 Corinthians 15:51-52). In the time it takes for the sound of the trumpet to fade away, it will all be over.

Living Now in Light of the Not Yet

If you are like me, you can't read these great promises of Scripture without asking, When exactly will all this happen? The answer is that Paul didn't know. God had not told him! The *fact* of Christ's coming is certain; the *time* of Christ's coming is a mystery known only by God. Paul believed that Christ could come during his life-time. He told the Thessalonians that he hoped to be among those still alive when Christ returned. He said, "*We* who are still alive and are left will be caught up" (1 Thessalonians 4:17, emphasis added). Don't be deceived by those who claim to have figured out when Jesus will return—and who want to sell you a book or a videotape that lets you in on the secret! God could have revealed the date of Jesus' coming as precisely as he revealed the order of events at his coming, but God has not chosen to do that. We are to live our lives as if Jesus could return for his people at any moment.

You may believe that after the rapture the world will be plunged into a period of chaos that will end only when Christ returns visibly to earth to set up a kingdom of righteousness. You may believe that the rapture will simply be part of the final end of human history. My purpose is not to debate the order of end-time events. What we should all be concerned with, regardless of our views on the events of the last days, is this challenge from the apostle John: "Dear children, continue in him, so that when he appears we may be confident and unashamed before him at his coming" (1 John 2:28). John adds later, "Everyone who has this hope [of Christ's return] in him purifies himself, just as he is pure" (1 John 3:3).

When I was a teenager, my parents would say to me before I

left home for an evening with my friends, "Go places where you could invite Christ to go and do things you would not be ashamed of doing if Christ were to return." I thought it was corny back then, but back then I wasn't very wise. Today it sounds like very good advice.

5

Thy Kingdom Come

"Yours, O LORD, is the greatness and the power
and the glory and the majesty and the splendor,
for everything in heaven and earth is yours.
Yours, O LORD, is the kingdom;
you are exalted as head over all.
Wealth and honor come from you;
you are ruler of all things.
In your hands are strength and power
to exalt and give strength to all.
Now, our God, we give you thanks,
and praise your glorious name."

1 CHRONICLES 29:11-13

*E**very fall my wife,* Karen, makes a Halloween costume for our son, Kyle. These are not the ordinary, just-like-everyone-else-has-on costumes. These are spectacular! A few years ago Kyle decided that he wanted to be a king. His robes and crown and jeweled scepter made him look like he had just stepped out of Buckingham Palace. The problem was he also liked pretending he had the authority of a king. He began to order food and snacks and bath water by snapping his fingers and barking orders at his loyal "subjects." The revolution came pretty fast that year, and we reminded Kyle that the king thing was only make-believe. He soon returned to his role as an ordinary boy, but being king for a while was fun.

It comes as a surprise to those of us who live under democratic forms of government that God's ideal form of human government is not embodied in the United States Congress or the British Parliament or the German Bundestag. God's ideal form of government is a kingdom ruled by one absolute monarch. The problem with earthly kings and queens and dictators is that the power of their office corrupts their hearts. They use their authority to oppress their people and persecute their enemies. But in God's ideal government the right person sits on the throne of power. God's King is the absolute sovereign, and everything he does is morally pure and ethically proper. He rules in "rightness" all the time. The King's name, of course, is Jesus.

Kingdom Life

One of the most powerful images of God's relationship to his own people is condensed in the phrase "the kingdom of God." During Israel's golden age in the Old Testament, God pictured his rule in the reigns of godly King David and David's son Solomon. Later, in the dark days of Israel's decline, God through his prophets promised a return to those golden days in a restored kingdom. When Jesus came on the scene, he told people in his generation that the kingdom was about to burst on the scene of human history. Jesus' closest followers fully expected after his resurrection that he would finally take control of this sinful, unjust world and would set up a glorious kingdom of peace.

Christians have written long, uninspiring books about the kingdom of God. They have debated when it will come and what it will be like and who gets in. It's too bad we have allowed the idea of God's kingdom to get bogged down in dry academic discussion. Most of us miss the power and grandeur of what the Bible says God's kingdom is all about.

" 'Already' the kingdom of Jesus has broken into the world.
He has accomplished a mighty victory over sin, death, and Satan
upon His cross. He has poured forth His Spirit,
and we are participating in the great harvest of men and women
as the gospel goes forth throughout the world.
But 'not yet' do we enjoy the fullness of the kingdom
and of life as it will only be known when King Jesus returns."
—SCOTTY SMITH and MICHAEL CARD

Some Christians conclude, based on their careful study of Scripture, that God's kingdom is fully operational right now. Wherever Jesus reigns as King, God's kingdom is functioning.

Since Christ reigns as Lord in the believer's life, we are inhabitants of the kingdom of God. Since Christ rules in the church, the Christian community is the visual expression of God's kingdom.

Other Christians believe that God's kingdom will be fully revealed in eternity. This world will come to an end when Jesus returns from heaven in glory. A new heaven and earth will then be created, and Jesus will reign as God's King forever.

Still other Christians conclude that Jesus will reign over a visible kingdom here on this earth. They believe that when Jesus returns, he will set up a kingdom of peace and abundance on this present earth for a thousand years (a millennium). Sin's curse will be lifted; disease will be eradicated; justice and harmony will prevail.

I think you can find biblical support for all three aspects of God's kingdom! There is a sense in which God has always and will always rule over his creation. The writer of Psalm 10 says, "The LORD is King for ever and ever" (Psalm 10:16). Daniel adds that "the Most High is sovereign over the kingdoms of men" (Daniel 4:17, 25, 32). Furthermore, Jesus, God the Son, has always ruled as King over the universe. Jesus was the Creator, and Jesus sustains his creation by his own power (Colossians 1:16-17; Hebrews 1:2-3).

There is also a sense in which we live every day under the rule of Jesus Christ. Christians are part of the kingdom of God because the King has come, and we have pledged our allegiance to him. It's not always obvious to those looking on, but Jesus does rule as King in his church. The body of believers you worship with should not look primarily to a denomination or church leader for direction. The church should seek to do what pleases the Lord, the sovereign King.

"Jesus emphasized that his true followers,
the citizens of God's kingdom, were to be entirely different from others.
They were not to take their cue from the people around them,
but from him." —JOHN R. W. STOTT

We've just about worn out the phrase "What would Jesus do?" but I think a lot of church squabbles would be settled if every believer would ask, "What would Jesus, the King, want me to do in this situation?" If gossip is passed to me, what response from me would please the King? If I see a brother or sister in need, what would the Lord of all I possess want me to sacrifice to help? I wonder if the people who come into my Christian community or into my home or who observe my life are able to see who the King of my life really is. The apostle Paul said that the marks of kingdom life are righteousness, peace and joy in the Holy Spirit (Romans 14:17). That *really* makes me wonder whether I live more like a citizen of a worldly kingdom than a citizen of the kingdom of God.

A Future New Millennium

As you read the Bible, you can't escape the fact that there is a present-day aspect to God's kingdom. But not everything God promises about his kingdom is fulfilled in our lives or in the church. The Old Testament prophets pictured God's kingdom as a time of worldwide peace and amazing prosperity. Sickness, aging, deformity and despair will be removed. War will be eliminated, and the industries of war will be turned to peaceful endeavors. Education and human creativity will reach undreamed heights. Arid, unproductive regions of the world will produce an abundance of food.[1] None of those incredible promises have been fulfilled even in a spiritual or figurative sense in the church or in our lives as Christians.

In addition to the clear promises of the Old Testament about an earthly kingdom, the apostle John in the book of Revelation sees Jesus returning to earth as "King of kings and Lord of lords" (Revelation 19:11-16). Jesus then sets up a kingdom over the whole earth. Six times in Revelation 20:1-7 John describes Jesus' reign as lasting one thousand years. Satan, the enemy of God's people, is bound so his deceptive work is removed from the earth. God's people reign with Christ over a renewed earth. All the blessings God has promised are fulfilled in the reign of God's perfect King—"the LORD will be King over the whole earth" (Zechariah 14:9).

Jesus himself talked about his future reign as God's righteous King. "When the Son of Man comes in his glory, and all the angels with him, he will sit on his throne in heavenly glory" (Matthew 25:31). Jesus' healing ministry was just a preview of the physical health that will mark God's future kingdom (Matthew 9:35; 10:7-8; 11:2-6). Before Christ's return in glory, the kingdom will grow silently and unobserved (Matthew 13:24-30), but at the end of the age Jesus is revealed as God's King and Jesus' faithful followers are ushered into the joy and blessing of God's kingdom (Matthew 13:43).

A Forever Kingdom

Jesus' reign over the kingdom of God for a thousand years doesn't tell the whole story either. When the angel Gabriel summarized her son's career for Mary, he said that Jesus would reign forever and that his kingdom would never end (Luke 1:33). Jesus' future earthly reign for a thousand years is just the first phase of the full expression of God's kingdom. At the end of the earthly reign of Christ, Satan will be released and will deceive a large group of people who have lived in a virtually perfect world. Those who rebel against Jesus the King will be destroyed, and Satan will be cast into the lake of fire (Revelation 20:7-10).

When the last of God's enemies is conquered by Jesus Christ, God will bring this present world to a fiery end (2 Peter 3:10-13).

Then, in an amazing act of power, God will bring a new heaven and new earth into existence (Isaiah 65:17; Revelation 21:1). God the Father and God the Son will reign together over a perfect kingdom of peace and joy forever. God's people from all the ages of earth's history will then enter "the *eternal* kingdom of our Lord and Savior Jesus Christ" (2 Peter 1:11, emphasis added). Jesus will reign for ever and ever.

So what we think of as heaven really has several stages to it. Today a believer in Christ who dies goes to the Father's house, the presence of Christ in heaven. During the future earthly reign of Christ for a thousand years, we will reign with him in his kingdom. Apparently we will live on the renewed earth in our resurrection bodies. But in eternity we will enjoy a totally *new* heaven and earth. Each stage brings new wonders and new opportunities, and yet each stage is marked by the greatest blessing of all—the visible, personal presence of Jesus.

Living Now in Light of Not Yet

It's wonderful to think about Christ's future kingdom or heaven's eternal kingdom, but God's promises about the future don't excuse us from kingdom living right now. Our efforts won't bring God's kingdom to earth, but we can certainly begin to live like kingdom subjects. If we were honest, most of us find it difficult to live kingdom lives. Part of the reason it's difficult is that everything under Christ's kingly rule is so different from the way things operate in the world around us. In the kingdoms of this world, power and money and recognition are the top prizes people struggle to obtain. We are men and women on the way up the corporate ladder. We want our share of whatever is out there.

When we check out the corporate policy of Jesus' kingdom, however, we find that the ideals are peace and right living. Profit always takes second place to people. Compassion is far more significant than competition.

Kingdom living also means making hard decisions and taking on risky responsibility. Living under Christ's kingship will push us out of our comfort zone in several areas of life. We can't singlehandedly eradicate poverty and hunger in our world like Jesus will in his future kingdom. But as kingdom subjects we can use what resources we have to help those who are poor or hungry or oppressed.

Christ's future kingdom will be marked by a restoration of the earth to the beauty and productiveness of its original creation. The shroud of sin that chokes the universe today will be lifted. If we as Christians are striving to live *today* as subjects of Christ the King, it seems to me that we will take our stewardship of the earth and its resources far more seriously.

Christians can't bring about worldwide racial harmony or eliminate racial bigotry from our culture like Jesus will in the kingdom. We can, however, build church communities where ethnic and racial barriers dissolve in the common bond of Jesus Christ.

Shocking stories of violence emerge every day in our world. Unfortunately, violence and drug abuse and child pornography will never be eradicated from human culture—until Jesus does it. But that future hope doesn't cause us to throw up our hands, for the present. We can still honor Christ the King by speaking and acting courageously against the elements that drag our society further and further from God's ideals of justice and peace.

Sorrow and heartache will continue to mark our path through life, but as kingdom subjects we can model what love and concern for others really mean. The world can't see Jesus the King or the magnificent splendor of his future kingdom on earth. All they can see are loyal kingdom subjects who try to live life in this age under the directives of the age to come.

Don't expect to get a lot of applause or recognition for living a kingdom life or for being involved in kingdom work. Following Jesus is like picking up a cross. We put our own priorities to death and we pattern our lives after our King—the one who came to serve, not to be served. Those who receive the highest honor in the culture of Christ's kingdom are the servants.

$\sim\!\!\backslash\!I\!/\!\!\sim$

6

Practicing Our Praise

"We praise Thee, O God:
We acknowledge Thee to be the Lord.
All the earth doth worship Thee, the Father everlasting."

TE DEUM
an early Christian hymn

I *thought it had been one of my best sermons.* In a series on worship we had looked at the magnificent scene in Revelation 4 and 5 where we see worship in heaven. Angels are shouting, elders are kneeling, the universe is ringing—and in the center of everything are God the Father and the Lamb, Jesus Christ. My heart had been lifted in joy and praise to the Lord.

As people made their way out of the church auditorium, I noticed one university student who remained seated in the pews. She was gazing at the front of the auditorium, lost in thought. A few minutes later I went over, sat beside her and asked her if I could help her in any way. "Is heaven just one endless church service?" she said. "Is this all we will do—just sing and kneel and look at God forever?" I had the distinct feeling that heaven didn't look very appealing to her at that moment.

I assured her that heaven would be much more than worship. Eternity will be filled with endless opportunities to enjoy every blessing of God to its fullest. But I also pointed out that God put this scene of worship in the Bible for a purpose. He wanted us to know that one of the main joys of heaven will be direct, face-to-face worship of the Lord.

Come Up Here!

Most of the book of Revelation centers on dire scenes of judgment and catastrophe. The chapters at the beginning of the book, however, (like the chapters at the end) give us an entirely different focus. In Revelation chapter 1 the apostle John sees Jesus in his majesty and glory. It's a sight that brings John to the ground in humility and adoration. He falls before the sovereign Lord of all creation. Some people are under the impression that when we get to heaven we will stroll up to Jesus and shake hands. Nothing could be further from the truth. We will fall before him as our Master and Lord.

> "Christians worship with a conviction that they
> are in the presence of God. Worship is an act of attention to the living God
> who rules, speaks and reveals, creates and redeems, orders and blesses.
> Outsiders, observing these acts of worship, see nothing like that.
> They see a few people singing unpopular songs,
> sometimes off-key, someone reading from an old book and making remarks
> that may or may not interest the listeners." —EUGENE PETERSON

After describing how Jesus looked, John wrote down what Jesus said. In Revelation 2 and 3 Jesus speaks to seven different churches. The churches represent Christian communities found everywhere. In the city where you live, there are "Ephesus"-type churches, for example. Maybe you attend one. Ephesus churches have an impressive history of service and dedication to the Lord. Their facilities are magnificent; their pastor has a long list of credentials; their weekly bulletin is crammed with activities and announcements. The only problem with an Ephesus church is that its people have lost their fervent love for Jesus. They are far more concerned about keeping the church machinery well-oiled than they are about pleasing Jesus Christ. They have stopped taking risks to advance God's kingdom. Jesus addresses seven different churches with commendation, rebuke and advice.

When Jesus finishes his messages to the churches, John's location changes. A voice from heaven says, "Come up here," and John is transported to heaven. From this point on in the book, every event on earth and in heaven is seen from heaven's perspective.

When John steps into heaven, a scene of incredible beauty unfolds in front of him. No video camera could record the brilliant lights and colors that burst open before John's eyes. No CD could reproduce the waves of sound and energy that wash over him. John himself struggles to find words that are adequate to describe what he experiences. You have to understand as you read these verses that God is communicating to us in drama. This is not like one of Paul's letters, where he teaches us certain facts like a teacher lecturing his students. God speaks to us here (and through much of the book of Revelation) in an unfolding dramatic presentation. It was designed to stir a sense of wonder and awe in our hearts. As you read, you find yourself not just listening but "seeing"; not just learning but wanting to participate. As angels shout, the same words rise to your lips. As believers kneel, you find yourself falling before God with them. These are chapters to be experienced as well as read and studied.

Three images capture John's attention. First he sees a throne and "someone sitting on it" (Revelation 4:2). John isn't told who is seated on the throne, but later the person is called "the Lord God Almighty" (Revelation 4:8). Obviously John saw a visible representation of God the Father. God the Father has no physical body. He is spirit and is not confined to one specific place like we are. God's glory and purity are portrayed in John's vision by brilliant light and the reflection of that light by precious stones.

The second image John sees is an arrangement of twenty-four additional thrones around the throne of God. The thrones are occupied by elders who are dressed in white and are crowned with golden crowns. These crowns are not diadems, the crowns of kings. These are victor's crowns, wreaths given to those who win in athletic games. The elders are human beings, God's own people, seated in heaven in glorified, resurrected bodies and rewarded for the faithfulness of their service and devotion to Christ. I am convinced that these elders represent Christians in heaven after our future resurrection.

Angels are the third image impressed on John's mind in this vision. Four magnificent, powerful living creatures are positioned around God's throne. They never stop exalting the awesomeness and eternal majesty of God.

> Holy, holy, holy
> is the Lord God Almighty,
> who was, and is, and is to come. (Revelation 4:8)

The elders are seated, but they don't stay in their seats. When the angelic quartet shouts praise to God, the elders, believers who have been redeemed and rewarded by God's grace, fall down and "worship him who lives for ever and ever" (Revelation 4:10). The crowns we have received for sacrificial devotion to Christ don't stay on our heads. We lay them before God's throne in gratitude and then take up the shout of praise and adoration to God.

Enter the Lamb

The worship scene continues into chapter five of Revelation, but the focus shifts from God the Father to God the Son. In the Father's hand is a scroll, spelling out in detail exactly how God will reclaim his creation from the grip of sin and death. God's original creation fell under a curse when Adam sinned, but now God is ready to reclaim what is rightfully his. The call goes out for someone who is capable of carrying out God's plan—but no one is found. No angel steps forward, no redeemed human being is capable. No one, it seems, has the power and the position necessary to bring God's redemptive plan to completion.

"Worship in the New Testament church is not simply practice
for some later heavenly experience of genuine worship,
nor is it simply pretending, or going through some outward activities.
It is genuine worship in the presence of God himself."—WAYNE GRUDEM

If you were listening to a sound track of Revelation 5, you would hear a loud voice calling for someone to open the scroll and carry out God's plan. Then you would hear a long silence as no one stepped forward. As the silence dragged on, you would hear an old man crying. John begins to weep. He's not crying just because he is curious and wants to see what's written on the scroll.

He is weeping because unless someone is found to open the scroll, God's plan will not be carried out. John is weeping because he wants God's kingdom to come and God's authority over creation to be restored. I have to ask myself as I read this, when was the last time I cried for an unredeemed world?

John turns away to weep, but one of the elders comes over to give him some good news. "Don't weep, John. I know someone who is worthy to open the scroll—the Lion of Judah, the Root of David" (Revelation 5:5, my paraphrase). John looks up to see the Lion and he sees a Lamb.

> Then I saw a Lamb, looking as if it had been slain, standing in the center of the throne, encircled by the four living creatures and the elders. (Revelation 5:6)

John sees a Lamb marked by violent death and yet standing in front of God's throne. This Lamb had triumphed over death and now was prepared to carry God's plan to completion. The "Lamb," of course, is Jesus Christ.

Jesus takes the scroll from God the Father and by that act signals the end of Satan's dominion and sin's stranglehold on God's creation. When God the Son takes the scroll and accepts the responsibility of reclaiming the world from sin's destructive power, the universe explodes in praise.

The wave begins with those closest to God's throne, the four

living creatures and God's redeemed people. They sing a new song
of blessing and adoration.

> You are worthy to take the scroll
>   and to open its seals,
> because you were slain,
>   and with your blood you purchased men for God
>   from every tribe and language and people and nation.
> You made them to be a kingdom and priests to serve our God,
>   and they will reign on the earth. (Revelation 5:9-10)

The hosts of angels are the next ones to join in. Millions of magnificent angelic beings add their voices.

> Worthy is the Lamb, who was slain,
> to receive power and wealth and wisdom and strength
> and honor and glory and praise! (Revelation 5:12)

Finally every creature in heaven and on earth blends in as one final shout of triumph rocks the universe.

> To him who sits on the throne and to the Lamb,
> be praise and honor and glory and power,
>   for ever and ever! (Revelation 5:13)

As the sound fades away, the four living creatures standing
around God's throne can only say "Amen"—meaning, "It's true!
Let it happen, Lord!" Those of us who have personally experi-

enced Jesus' power to redeem those who were lost and beyond hope will have nothing to add. We will simply fall on our faces before the Savior and worship him (Revelation 5:14).

Living Now in Light of the Not Yet

I think one of the reasons we struggle with the idea of worship in heaven is that we find worship on earth so routine, so predictable. We gather with other believers and say we have come together to worship God, but if we are honest, we are focused far more on ourselves than on the Lord. We've fallen into the trap of thinking that we are the audience in worship and that the performers are the professionals up front. Nothing will kill the spirit of genuine worship more effectively than sitting in a comfortable seat, just watching the show and waiting to get something out of a church service.

The only audience in worship is God. He is the one we are gathered to honor and praise and exalt. His character, his goodness, his grace and mercy and forgiveness are the focus of true worship. Those of us sitting in the pews or standing on the stage are the performers. Our single goal is to please our Audience. The crunch is that we can't just bluff our way through our performance. The Audience we are striving to please is not impressed with the outward motions of worship. He is impressed with the attitude of our hearts before him and with the sacrifice we offer of our praise to him.

I wonder what would happen to our worship as a Christian community if, as we put on clean clothes on Sunday for church, we were just as concerned that our hearts were clean and presentable before the Lord. I wonder if our worship would be more stirring and life-changing if, when we sang songs of praise, we envisioned ourselves singing directly to God and not to ourselves or to other people. I wonder what it would do to the average congregation if we came together not to get something for ourselves but to give God the honor he alone deserves. I think we would find our own needs being met and our own hearts transformed as we turned our attention to the only person worthy of acclaim.

Something else from this heavenly vision concerns me. The worship scene John saw in heaven is not what we witness in most churches on a typical Sunday morning. John saw God's people "from every tribe and language and people and nation" (Revelation 5:9-10). We haven't been very effective in building multiracial Christian communities, even in cities peppered with different racial and ethnic people. Churches tend to be made up of single ethnic groups. It would help, I think, if we would at least consciously realize that when we gather for worship, we are joining in spirit with brothers and sisters in Christ of every racial group to exalt the Lord. Maybe that would make us more willing to invite and welcome people who are different from us into our Christian fellowship and even into our personal circle of friends.

One other perspective from these chapters in Revelation has helped me as I've gathered with other Christians for worship. The church you attend may be very small or very large—or somewhere in-between. The style of your worship service may be open and spontaneous or more traditional. What will lift you beyond the routine of worship is realizing that as you raise your voice in praise to God, you are joining not simply with brothers and sisters around the world, you are also joining with the hosts of angels and the multitudes of believers already in heaven in lifting up the one true God. The Father is worthy of our worship, the Son is worthy of our honor, the Spirit is worthy of our praise. If you want to be bored, be bored with the stock market reports or the latest political scandal, but never be bored with worship.

"What, then, is the essence of worship?
It is the celebration of God!
When we worship God, *we celebrate Him*:
we extol Him, we sound His praises, we boast in Him."
—RONALD ALLEN and GORDON BORROR

Jesus is not in Bethlehem in a manger anymore, although a lot of people would like to keep him there. He's not wandering the hills of Palestine teaching people and doing good deeds, although plenty of people see him that way. Jesus is not on the cross any more either—or in a tomb. He's in heaven, alive and in the middle of everything God plans to do. He is there as our conquering Lord. He is worthy of all our adoration forever. The young woman who was afraid heaven would be nothing more than an endless church service has nothing to fear. Eternity will not be long enough to sing and shout the Savior's praises. We will never get tired of being in his presence. New works of God's grace call for new songs of joyful adoration—and those songs will never end.

7

Run to Win

"In mansions of glory and endless delight,
I'll ever adore Thee in heaven so bright;
I'll sing with the glittering crown on my brow,
If ever I loved Thee, my Jesus, 'tis now."

WILLIAM FEATHERSTONE

I am convinced that if the apostle Paul were on earth today, he would be an avid sports fan. He would enjoy ESPN, the World Series and the Super Bowl. Most of all, Paul would look forward to the Olympic Games, particularly the great feats of endurance and strength like the marathon and decathlon.

Paul was attracted to athletic games because they were such powerful illustrations of the Christian life. Paul was intimately aware of the price that had to be paid to be a genuine competitor. He had watched athletes train. He had studied the habits of the athletes who succeeded and the habits of those who failed. Paul drew stunning parallels between the discipline needed for athletic competition and the endurance required to live the Christian life. Both endeavors call for an intense, single-minded focus on winning. Both demand hard work and rigorous training. At the end of the Christian life, just like at the end of an athletic event, those who have run with endurance receive a reward.

Most of us, when we think about heaven, picture the end of pain and suffering, or a happy reunion with friends and family members who have died or been welcomed into the presence of Christ. What most of us don't think about much in relation to heaven is standing before Jesus to give an account of our lives — and to receive rewards from his hands. If you are like me, just being in heaven seems enough of a reward, but Paul knew that our entrance into heaven also involved an evaluation of our lives by Jesus himself.

Receiving Christ's Reward

Jesus' evaluation of us will not be to see if we are saved or lost. That issue was settled when we believed in him and received eternal life by his grace alone. Instead, we will face an evaluation of how we used the gifts and opportunities God gave us. The results of Christ's evaluation will bring us either reward or loss of reward.

Some Christians object to the whole idea of rewards for our faith-ful service to Christ. After I spoke on future rewards at a Bible con-ference, a man bulldozed his way to the front of the auditorium to tell me that he didn't need rewards to serve Christ. "I serve the Lord out of love, not to get a reward!" His words came from a genuine sense of gratitude to Christ, and I told him how much I admired his spirit of servanthood. But then I reminded him that Jesus talked a lot about rewards in heaven—and so did Paul and John in the New Testa-ment. Our future rewards are another example of God's gracious de-sire to give abundantly to those he loves. If you treat those promised rewards lightly, you are looking down on some of God's greatest gifts.

> "Heaven's rewards are all a matter of God's grace.
> They are God's generous recognition of selfless
> and sacrificial service." — J. OSWALD SANDERS

Other Christians get nervous about comparing the Christian life to athletic competition. The writers of the New Testament, however, had no problem picturing the Christian's time on earth as a race or a wrestling match or a bout in the boxing ring (1 Corinthians 9:24-26; Ephesians 6:12; 2 Timothy 4:7; Hebrews 12:1). What will help you keep the right perspective is to realize that the idea of competition against other Christians is *not* part of the New Testament teaching. We are striving individually to please one Master. We are competing only against ourselves to grow in our faithfulness to the Lord and our willingness to sacrifice ourselves for his glory.

The clearest statements about our future evaluation come from the apostle Paul.

Why do you judge your brother? Or why do you look down on your brother? For we will all stand before God's judgment seat. . . . Each of us will give an account of himself to God. (Romans 14:10, 12)

So we make it our goal to please [the Lord]. . . . For we must all appear before the judgment seat of Christ, that each one may receive what is due him, for the things done while in the body, whether good or bad." (2 Corinthians 5:9-10)

If the thought of standing before Christ to give an account of your life strikes terror in your heart, remember that there is no condemnation waiting for those who are in Christ (Romans 8:1). If you have received Jesus Christ as Savior and Lord, he is not sitting in heaven with a club in his hand. Jesus already suffered the wrath of God that we deserved. His future evaluation of our lives (like all of his acts toward us) is a demonstration of his love—and his perfect love drives all fear away.

What's the Agenda?

When I go into a meeting, particularly a meeting that focuses on me in some way, I like to know what is going to be discussed. Most Christians are surprised by the list of issues Jesus will cover with each one of us when we stand before him.

Works. We are saved by grace apart from any works of our own. But once we have been born again, we are called to live obedient, faithful lives. Every deed, every word we've spoken, will come under the scrutiny of Jesus. The apostle Paul pictures us as construction workers on a lifelong project.

> By the grace God has given me, I laid a foundation as an expert builder, and someone else is building on it. But each one should be careful how he builds. For no one can lay any foundation other than the one already laid, which is Jesus Christ. If any man builds on this foundation using gold, silver, costly stones, wood, hay or straw, his work will be shown for what it is, because the Day will bring it to light. It will be revealed with fire, and the fire will test the quality of each man's work. If what he has built survives, he will receive his reward. If it is burned up, he will suffer loss; he himself will be saved, but only as one escaping through the flames. (1 Corinthians 3:10-15)

I carry several important truths away from that passage. What's most important to remember is that our works have value only if they are built on the foundation of Jesus Christ. But on that foundation a Christian can build with two kinds of materials—materials that will survive Christ's evaluation and those that won't.

Actions motivated by pride or self-glory are compared to wood, hay or straw. It's possible to do very religious things like pray or give to people in need or teach the Bible or sing a solo out of a desire to exalt ourselves and to receive the praise of other people. Those works and the motives behind them will be exposed and burned up. On the other hand, works motivated by love for God and a sincere desire to please him, works prompted by our pursuit of the will of God, will be revealed as objects of incredible worth—gold, silver and costly stones.

If you are a Christian, you *are* building a building whether you realize it or not. Every day at work or in your home or browsing the Web you are choosing materials to put in that structure. Be careful how you build.

Hidden things. Paul touches on another item on Jesus' evaluation agenda in 1 Corinthians 4:5.

> Therefore judge nothing before the appointed time; wait till the Lord comes. He will bring to light what is hidden in darkness and will expose the motives of men's hearts. At that time each will receive his praise from God.

I don't think Paul means that every sin we've ever committed will be dredged up for all to see. When we confess our sins, God forgives those sins. They are removed from us forever. What Paul is talking about are the issues in our lives that are hidden and that we would like to keep that way—the underhanded moves against a fellow employee, the subtle manipulation of our spouse or children, the sharing of a "need" in someone else's life designed to put that person down, the power play on the church committee. The things we've kept secret and never truly resolved will some day be fully exposed.

"Someday, time will run out. . . . And I will go in a box.
The box has a trick bottom;
I tumble through it into something beyond words,
beyond time, charged with light, light of a scorching love
that will burn away so much of what I now excuse,
deny, rationalize. Then I will be called to give an account
for every careless word I uttered, and every irreplaceable moment
I wasted."—FREDERICA MATHEWES-GREEN

Jesus will not bring those issues to light simply to embarrass us. He will bring them to light so we will resolve the issues in the way he told us to resolve them. If I stand before the Lord with a history of unconfessed sin in my life on earth, he will see to it that I deal with that openly before him before I enter heaven's glory. Jesus would prefer, of course, that I deal with unconfessed sin now, before I give an account to him. But if I refuse to obey him today, he will call me on it in the future.

When I was a young seminary student, I worked in a church as a youth pastor. A conflict arose with one set of parents that was never resolved. I can honestly say that I tried at the time to come to some reconciliation with them, but they were too angry to settle the issue, and they left the church. I believe that if this rupture in fellowship between us is not dealt with in this life, the three of us will have to deal with it at Jesus' feet. I hope that prospect motivates you to check through the closets of your life and to put right the issues and relationships that are wrong. The other people involved may have forgotten all about it, but God keeps extremely accurate records.

Leadership in the church. If you have a position of responsibility and authority in the church, there's a special section on Jesus' evaluation form just for you. Those of us who lead God's people will give an account to Christ for our care of his people (Hebrews 13:17). We will answer for our attitudes and actions toward people in our congregations or the children in our kid's program or the praise team members we direct or the single parents we try to encourage. Responsibility in the church is not something to be taken lightly.

The use of our resources. The Holy Spirit has given every believer spiritual gifts that we are to use in ministry to the body of Christ, and we will give an account for the use (or nonuse—or misuse) of those gifts. Our use of time and energy and especially money will come under close scrutiny in our evaluation before the Lord of all we possess. Jesus made it clear that we are to use our resources to do good and to help those in need.

Sell your possessions and give to the poor. Provide purses for your-
selves that will not wear out, a treasure in heaven that will not be ex-
hausted, where no thief comes near and no moth destroys. For where
your treasure is, there your heart will be also. (Luke 12:33-34)

What will Jesus find as he flips through your checkbook or Visa
statement? Where we spend our money quickly reveals where our
heart is focused.

Vindication. The judgment seat of Christ will also reveal a Christian's faithfulness and obedience to God. Some pastors or church
leaders who have been wrongly treated will be shown to be faithful servants of Christ. Christians who have suffered persecution
will be honored. Missionaries who have worked in remote areas
with little response to the message of Christ and with little recognition for their sacrifice and ministry will hear praise and acclaim
from Jesus himself.

It's easy to look at other Christians and to pass judgment on
their actions or lack of involvement in the things we think are important, but two key facts should keep our minds and attitudes on
track. First, we won't give an account to Christ for anyone else's
building, only our own. The other fact to remember is that only
the fire of Jesus' appraisal will reveal the true value of a person's
work. Some people who always seem to be in the religious spot-
light may in that future day be exposed as self-centered frauds.
Other people who seem to have an insignificant place in God's

program may be revealed to have lived lives of unselfish, unwavering devotion to Christ.

Crowned with Honor

At the end of our evaluation we will either receive rewards from Christ or we will suffer the loss of reward (1 Corinthians 3:14-15). The victor in an ancient athletic event received a crown, a ring of branches woven together and placed on his head. The crown symbolized the years of sacrifice and training that the athlete had invested in preparation. The crown also carried additional honors and privileges. The winning athlete was exempt from taxes and military duty for life. He was honored in his community from that day forward.

The rewards Jesus will give are most often pictured in the Bible as "crowns." Christians who have served Christ faithfully will receive some visible token of reward and honor. The crown of life, for example, is promised to those who endure persecution and trial (James 1:12; Revelation 2:10). The apostle Paul anticipated receiving the crown of righteousness that is promised to every Christian who is faithful to Christ until death or until Jesus returns (2 Timothy 4:8). Church leaders who watch over God's people as tender shepherds will receive a crown of glory that will never tarnish or decay (1 Peter 5:4). Those who exercise discipline and commitment in their Christian lives will receive "a crown that will last forever" (1 Corinthians 9:25). Jesus will not overlook the smallest act of kindness done in his name (Mark 9:41).

"Death closes the door on making amends,
opens the door to a flood of 'If only . . .' thoughts."—JOSEPH BAYLY

Committed athletes devote every ounce of strength to reaching one goal. They want to win. Christians are called to put that same effort and discipline into pleasing and obeying Christ. Athletes compete for a symbol of honor that perishes. The ancient laurel crowns have all dissolved into dust. In time, Super Bowl rings and the Stanley Cup trophy will crumble. But the crowns we will receive are imperishable. They never tarnish or decay. No one will truck them off to a museum or auction them off after we die. The honor and acclaim we receive from Jesus will ring in our ears for eternity.

The sad part is that not every Christian will receive a crown. Some will suffer the loss of their reward (1 Corinthians 3:15). I don't think that means that Jesus will give us a reward and then snatch it back. I think it means we will be allowed to see the reward that *could* have been ours if we had been fully committed to Christ, if we had chosen our building materials more carefully, if our motives had been focused on God's glory and not on our own glory. Some of us will suffer shame when we stand before the

Lord (1 John 2:28). God will wipe away all tears in heaven but not before hot tears of remorse and confession mark the faces of those who have taken lightly the serious commands of God's Word.

The apostle Paul had one fear as he thought about the future day of evaluation before Christ. He did not want to be responsible for calling so many other people into the race of the Christian life and then do something that would disqualify him from receiving a crown of his own. "I beat my body and make it my slave so that after I have preached to others, I myself will not be disqualified for the prize" (1 Corinthians 9:27). Paul did not think he would lose his salvation. What struck dread in his heart was losing his reward. In Paul's mind the future rewards that God promised were powerful motivators to a life of obedience to Christ.

Living Now in Light of the Not Yet
Motivation for obedience to Christ is exactly where this whole discussion of our future rewards should grab each one of us. Why *do* you follow Christ and seek to honor him as Lord? Most of us would say that we follow Christ first of all because we love him. He paid the price of our sin. Before we ever began to seek him, he was seeking us. Who wouldn't want to follow a Savior like Jesus? God himself is a great reward, and knowing God personally fulfills the deepest longings and desires of the human heart. Love for

Christ is certainly the primary motive for serving him.

But God in his grace also promises rewards to those who serve him. I've heard some Christians treat those rewards pretty casually, as if God's promises were insignificant. As you read the New Testament, however, you quickly discover that the biblical writers weren't casual about future rewards. Paul and Peter and John were striving to gain Christ's approval on their work and on their lives.

If you want to sense what that future evaluation before Christ will be like—and if you are courageous enough to face the truth about yourself—carve out some time in the next few days for some personal examination. In your journal or a small notebook, list every major arena of your life: career, marriage, children, friends, church life, personal time, thought life. Imagine yourself standing in front of the Lord, who sees every thought and motive clearly, and practice giving an account of each area of your life. Do you behave at work, for example, as if Jesus was your boss? Are your attitudes at home consistent with your claim to be following Christ? Would you be comfortable if Jesus were sitting next to you as you surf the Internet or pick out videos? What would Jesus say about how you spend your money—or about how you give to him? As you honestly evaluate each area, write down the things that will prompt praise from the Lord. Then write down the issues that will bring loss of reward. Be sure to give yourself time to listen to the Spirit's commendation—and conviction—in each area.

The purpose of this spiritual exercise is not to discourage you. It is designed to motivate you to get back into the race with renewed enthusiasm. If your building project has been going poorly, tear out the worthless materials by confession and restitution and then rebuild those sections with actions and motives that honor Christ.

Jesus will give us these wonderful crowns of reward, but we won't wear them long. When we stand redeemed and rewarded before God, we will fall down in worship and awe before him and lay our crowns at his feet (Revelation 4:10). In the end we will realize that our greatest reward is God himself. I can't help but wonder, though, what it would be like to kneel before a God of such love, a God who has given so much to me, and have nothing of beauty to give back to him. I've had to face times of great shame in my life, but I can't imagine a more overwhelming shame than to stand before Jesus' nail-pierced hands with empty hands.

8

Working for Your Father

"Give me the love that leads the way,
The faith that nothing can dismay,
The hope no disappointments tire,
The passion that will burn like fire.
Let me not sink to be a clod;
Make me Thy fuel, Flame of God."

AMY CARMICHAEL

I learned to work from my father. He taught his three children to start a job promptly, to stay with the job diligently and to finish well. Whatever we lacked in motivation or enthusiasm, my dad willingly supplied. In my younger years I wasn't very happy about my father's work ethic, but I've seen his instruction pay multiple rewards as an adult. The habit of faithfully carrying through on small things has opened doors to greater responsibilities and more satisfying rewards.

Most Christians understand that we are to be involved in God's work here on earth. Part of our responsibility to the God who cleansed us from sin is to serve him. We don't serve the Lord in order to *be* saved; we serve him because we have *been* saved. If Christ sacrificed himself to give us life, how can we do less than offer ourselves back to him in gratitude? We present ourselves to God as living sacrifices to be consumed in doing what he desires (Romans 12:1-2).

Most of us don't think about the fact that our part in God's future program will be a reflection of how faithfully we do God's work today. When our lives are evaluated by Jesus Christ, we will first receive crowns of reward. But we will also get a new assignment based on what we did with the gifts and opportunities Christ gives us today.

Investing the Master's Money

In the middle of a long sermon about his future return from heaven to usher in God's kingdom, Jesus told an instructive story about a wealthy man who was leaving on a journey. Since he wouldn't be able to manage his assets personally, the man entrusted his money to three servants. He gave more than half his money to the servant who had been with him the longest and who had proven himself most capable of handling such a large responsibility. Five talents of money was an incredible sum. The word *talents* used in this parable refers to a large weight of gold or silver.

One talent represented an average worker's salary for twenty years! Do the math based on your own salary and you have some idea of the funds the first slave had at his disposal.

The second servant in the story received two talents of money and the third servant just one talent. Then the wealthy businessman left on his journey, and the servants went to work managing the master's funds.

The man who had received the five talents went at once and put his money to work and gained five more. So also, the one with the two talents gained two more. But the man who had received the one talent went off, dug a hole in the ground and hid his master's money. (Matthew 25:16-18)

When the master returned, he called in each servant and asked for an accounting of his money. We get to listen in on each one's performance review.

The man who had received the five talents brought the other five. "Master," he said, "you entrusted me with five talents. See, I have gained five more."

His master replied, "Well done, good and faithful servant! You have been faithful with a few things; I will put you in charge of many things. Come and share your master's happiness!"

The man with the two talents also came. "Master," he said, "you entrusted me with two talents; see, I have gained two more."

His master replied, "Well done, good and faithful servant! You have been faithful with a few things; I will put you in charge of many things. Come and share your master's happiness!" (Matthew 25:20-23)

I'm disappointed that Jesus left so much out of this story. We aren't told, for example, *how* the two servants doubled their master's money. Obviously they invested the money wisely and saw an abundant return. Today they could write a best-selling book and open an Internet site on how to double your money in just a few months. We would all like to cash in on their investment strategy, but Jesus doesn't reveal any of their secrets.

> "To 'be ready' for Christ's return
> is to be faithfully obeying him in the present,
> actively engaged in whatever work
> he has called us to do." —WAYNE GRUDEM

I'm surprised even more that the master doesn't bother to ask the servants how they did it. He just praises them for their accomplishment. In spite of the difference in the size of their return, the master gives both servants the same honor—"Well done, good and faithful servant!" The rich man also increases each servant's responsibility. They had been faithful at one level of responsibility and that prepared them for a greater level. Finally the rich man gave each of them a share in the profits. They were invited to enter into their master's happiness.

The first two servants were in and out of the evaluation session in a flash. They demonstrated their resourcefulness, the master gave his commendation, and they walked out with a promotion and a bonus. Just the kind of performance evaluation we all dream about!

Servant number three, however, had some explaining to do.

Then the man who had received the one talent came. "Master," he said, "I knew that you are a hard man, harvesting where you have not sown and gathering where you have not scattered seed. So I was afraid and went out and hid your talent in the ground. See, here is what belongs to you."

His master replied, "You wicked, lazy servant! So you knew that I harvest where I have not sown and gather where I have not scattered seed? Well then, you should have put my money on deposit with the bankers, so that when I returned I would have received it back with interest.

"Take the talent from him and give it to the one who has the ten talents. For everyone who has will be given more, and he will have an abundance. Whoever does not have, even what he has will be taken from him. And throw that worthless servant outside, in the darkness, where there will be weeping and gnashing of teeth." (Matthew 25:24-30)

We already know that this servant was the least productive of the three because the master put him in charge of the smallest amount of money. You would think that he would have seen the master's action as an opportunity to prove himself. Instead he convinced himself that the master was making unrealistic, even impossible demands. This was a hard boss to please! When you first read this, it sounds like the man lived in such fear of the master that he did the only safe thing he could think of—he hid the money. Poor guy! He was paralyzed by his master's demands and ended up biting his nails until the master returned.

Before you buy this servant's story of victimization, however, you need to listen to the master's evaluation. He characterizes the man as wicked and lazy. The story the servant tried to pass off as an excuse for his inaction was a lie! The servant made up his excuses while he was swinging in a hammock—or swinging a golf club. The master even pointed out the fatal flaw in the servant's testimony. If he knew the master to be so demanding, at least he could have put the money in the bank and earned a little interest. The master might have accepted the "I-was-too-afraid" line if the servant had at least done that much. But the servant was too lazy to even carry the money to the bank. He dug a hole, dropped it in and then took a nap to restore his energy.

What we aren't quite prepared for is the master's judgment. After his stinging rebuke the master takes away the money the servant was given in the first place and gives it to the man overseeing ten talents. He then banishes the lazy servant from the celebration of the master's return. He is outside, consumed with regret and shame.

A Little Self-Examination

This story Jesus told is not difficult to understand. The painful part is applying its truth to our everyday lives. Obviously those of us who claim to be Christians are the servants in the passage, and Jesus is the master who has left on a long journey. When Jesus returns, he will ask each one of us for an accounting.

Jesus purposely designed this parable to make us a little uncomfortable. Several issues gnaw away at us as the story ends.

Giving an account. The accounting itself is one of them. Most of us glide through life relying on God's grace to save us, and we give very little thought to any future evaluation. It makes us nervous to think very long about standing before the Lord and giving an account of our lives. But Jesus left no doubt that a day of evaluation is coming.

My personal gifts. Another fact we have to face as we read this parable is that God has entrusted us with different levels of giftedness. We all receive spiritual gifts that we are to invest in ministry, but some of us are five-talent servants, some are two-talent servants and some are one-talent servants. That's not a cause for jealousy, because the gifts are the Master's to give as he desires. What he looks for is faithfulness in using those gifts. He doesn't tell us in detail how we are to invest our gifts. He just expects a return on what he has entrusted to us. The servants who doubled the master's money had to approach their task with the intention of seeing the money grow. They had to take some risks. I don't know precisely what their strategy was, but I can guarantee that they didn't just sit around and wait for a hot investment to drop into their laps.

Most Christians, I'm afraid, have no strategy at all for using their ministry gifts. We can't even tell someone else what our areas of giftedness are. Instead of setting out to find our gifts by investing ourselves in opportunities for ministry, we wait until someone begs us to do something. Even then we want to know how long we have to commit to the task and what the process is to get out of it if it's too difficult or inconvenient. We are like the third servant who just buried the master's gift.

No excuses. The most disturbing fact to emerge from Jesus' story is that the Master will immediately see through all our fabrications and excuses. When opportunities to serve others in the body of Christ present themselves, some of us are experts at coming up with excuses for not getting involved. I wonder how those excuses will sound in Jesus' ears. We think that Jesus will just overlook our failure to use the gifts and resources he has given us. We've convinced ourselves that he will say, "That's okay; I understand. I wasn't really serious about dedicated service anyway." That's what the third servant thought too. He found himself on the outside with the master's rebuke ringing in his ears. I don't think that means the third servant was kicked out of heaven. He just missed the opportunity for greater responsibility (and greater reward) in the future kingdom.

Living Now in Light of the Not Yet

Jesus must have liked this story because he told several different versions of it. The story changed depending on the audience and circumstances. In Luke's Gospel, Jesus says that the rich man chose ten servants and entrusted each with the same amount of money (one mina—about three month's wages). When the master returned, each servant was required to give an account of how the gift was used. One servant shrewdly invested the money and had ten minas to give back to the master. Another had worked hard but had received only five minas of return. Each one was rewarded. The servant who gained ten minas was put in charge of ten cities, and the servant who gained five minas found himself governing five cities. (The account is in Luke 19:12-27.)

I think this version adds one more important fact to our understanding of how our faithfulness today affects our future. In the future kingdom of God on earth, Christians will reign with Jesus

Christ (1 Corinthians 6:2-3; Revelation 20:6). We will be responsible to oversee the kingdom in some way. Those who have been faithful and intentional about investing their gifts and resources in God's work in this age will have even greater responsibility given to them in that future age. Those who commit themselves to sacrificial involvement in service to the body of Christ now may find themselves ruling cities then. Dedicated work is rewarded by more work and greater opportunity to serve the King. Jesus told his followers more than once that those who are faithful with a little thing will be faithful with much (Luke 16:10; 19:17). The faithful servants in the parable were not sent into retirement but given even more challenging tasks to fill their time.

> "In heaven we will not spend our time sitting on the edge
> of a cloud or playing a harp. . . .
> We will be busier than we have ever been."—JOHN MACARTHUR

Heaven will be a place of rest but not retirement. We will have plenty of fascinating, fulfilling things to do and an eternity to do them. Work is not a curse (even though we feel that way most Monday mornings). Work is a blessing we will pursue even after this life. I hope that fact sheds some new perspective on your work today. You aren't just punching the clock to pay the rent. You are working to please your boss—your *real* boss, Jesus Christ (Colossians 3:23-24).

The other side of the picture is that some of us will be sitting on the sidelines in the kingdom, warming the bench. Jesus' story in Luke had a lazy servant too. He hid his money just like his counterpart in Matthew. The master takes what little the lazy servant has and gives it to the one who had earned ten minas. The first servant now creatively rules eleven cities and the tenth servant finds himself unemployed.

You are in both versions of this parable. So am I. We could write our names above one of the servant's descriptions. We just have to decide which servant we really are—and what we are going to do about it.

Some people have tried to read the process of salvation into these parables. They think Jesus is saying that we have to pile up good works to be saved or to make it to heaven, but that's not what Jesus is trying to communicate. All the participants already are servants of the master. The master evaluates them on what they did with the resources they had been given. Every Christian is a child of God and a servant of Christ by grace alone. What Jesus will look for at that future evaluation is what we did with all that he entrusted to us—our time, our abilities, our money, our opportunities. It might be an interesting exercise to write out a rough draft of how you think your evaluation session would go if Jesus returned today. Don't try to inflate your accomplishments or make excuses for your failures, because Jesus will see right through them. In fact, if you ask the Lord to give you a preliminary evaluation and you listen quietly to what he says, it won't take you long to get a very clear picture of where you stand with him right now—and there's still time to put what he has entrusted to you to work.

Maybe as you allow God to evaluate your life, you will sense his affirmation and approval. Be encouraged by that! Don't focus on the lazy third servant so much that you forget the first two servants, who received the master's commendation. To my disappointment, I sometimes meet loving, committed Christians who fear facing the Lord. They fear that we will stand before Christ in guilt and imperfection to be rebuked and criticized. They picture Jesus playing a videotape of their lives and pausing the action often to point out every flaw and failure. That is *not* our future.

"We have lost a sense of heaven
and therefore have lost a sense of how this life is to be lived
for eternal impact."—HOWARD HENDRICKS

We will stand before Christ clothed in purity and covered in grace. The little New Testament book of Jude assures us that we will be presented to Christ "without fault and with great joy" (Jude 24). Jesus' delight will be to honor us with his praise.

One verse that keeps me from focusing too much on my failures and not enough on faithfulness is Hebrews 6:10—"God is not unjust; he will not forget your work and the love you have shown him as you have helped his people and continue to help them." Are you laboring in a difficult job but consistently try to honor Jesus as Lord? God will not forget. Have you stayed in a marriage when it would have been far easier to bail out? God will not forget. Are you faithfully serving God and no one seems to notice how well? God will not forget. The day will come when the hard work of commitment will return to you multiple times as you hear words of appreciation from Jesus himself. No song ever sung, no prayer spoken, no witness shared, no deed done in his name, no gift given will pass his notice. Your faithful devotion to Christ may go unrecognized and unappreciated here, but someday you will receive the Master's approval—and that will be far better than any applause on earth.

$\sim\!\!\backslash\!/\!\!\sim$
9

Welcome to the Party!

*"If you're not allowed to laugh in heaven,
I don't want to go there."*

MARTIN LUTHER

A friend of mine who has several active children told me that he was looking forward to heaven just to get a little peace and quiet. I think most Christians envision heaven as a serious, quiet place—like an enormous cathedral where conversations are held in whispers and the soft strains of the choir float through the hallways.

When we come to the Bible, however, we find a very different picture. In the book of Revelation heaven is a place filled with shouts, resounding songs, loud voices from loud angels, trumpet blasts and the rumble of thunder. If you are looking for quiet organ music and the hushed silence of a library in heaven, you will be disappointed.

When Jesus talked about the future, he pictured it most often as a party! Jesus was criticized regularly during his earthly ministry for having too much fun. The uptight religious people called Jesus a drunkard and a friend of low-class sinners. Even the followers of John the Baptizer were scandalized that Jesus didn't require his disciples to put on sad faces and skip meals. Jesus enjoyed banquets and parties on earth because they reminded him so much of heaven—and because they provided wonderful opportunities to teach people how the social rules will change when Jesus is in charge.

Jesus at the Table

A little plaque hung on the wall over my grandmother's kitchen table, welcoming Jesus to the table as an unseen guest. I often wondered as a child what it would be like if Jesus really did show up for a meal. Then I opened the Bible and found out that it might not be such a pleasant experience!

At one banquet that Jesus attended, he watched the guests pour into the dining room and rush for the most visible seats and the tables closest to the buffet line. In the middle of all the commotion, Jesus started to confront the guests about their rude behavior. It wasn't his house or his party, but he said what needed to be said.

> When someone invites you to a wedding feast, do not take the place of
> honor, for a person more distinguished than you may have been in-
> vited. If so, the host who invited both of you will come and say to you,
> "Give this man your seat." Then, humiliated, you will have to take the
> least important place. But when you are invited, take the lowest place,
> so that when your host comes, he will say to you, "Friend, move up to
> a better place." Then you will be honored in the presence of all your
> fellow guests. For everyone who exalts himself will be humbled, and
> he who humbles himself will be exalted. (Luke 14:8-11)

The guests who had pushed their way to the honored seats sat
red-faced with embarrassment. The host of the party didn't know
what to do, but before he could say anything, Jesus called him on
the carpet too.

> When you give a luncheon or dinner, do not invite your friends,
> your brothers or relatives, or your rich neighbors; if you do, they
> may invite you back and so you will be repaid. But when you give a
> banquet, invite the poor, the crippled, the lame, the blind, and you
> will be blessed. Although they cannot repay you, you will be repaid
> at the resurrection of the righteous. (Luke 14:12-14)

Maybe it was best that Jesus was the *unseen* guest at my grandmother's table! The appetizers hadn't even been served, and Jesus
had already exposed the selfishness of the guests and the hypoc-

risy of the host. The guests came only to see and be seen, and the host invited only the people who could be counted on to return the invitation. I think there was a long, awkward silence as everyone stared at Jesus in shocked embarrassment.

Finally one of the guests tried to break the tension with a worn-out, pious response to an awkward situation. He said, "Blessed is the man who will eat at the feast in the kingdom of God" (Luke 14:15). In other words, "Won't it be wonderful when we get to heaven, and we won't have to put up with this kind of embarrassment!" Obviously the man thought he was going to be one of the guests in God's future kingdom, and he was hoping that Jesus wouldn't be there to spoil the fun.

The Rest of the Story
That comment from the crowd prompted Jesus to tell a story.

A certain man was preparing a great banquet and invited many guests. At the time of the banquet he sent his servant to tell those who had been invited, "Come, for everything is now ready."

But they all alike began to make excuses. The first said, "I have just bought afield, and I must go and see it. Please excuse me."

Another said, "I have just bought five yoke of oxen, and I'm on my way to try them out. Please excuse me."

Still another said, "I just got married, so I can't come." (Luke 14:16-20)

What you have to understand as you read this account is that all these guests had already been invited to the banquet and had made a commitment to attend. They knew that the banquet would be on a certain day. The servant's personal call was simply to inform them that the banquet was ready.

"The angels know what the joys of heaven are,
and therefore, they rejoice over one sinner
who repents."—CHARLES SPURGEON

The shocking part of the story to the people in Jesus' culture was that each of the invited guests refused to come—and they gave such flimsy excuses. Who buys a piece of property without looking at it first? Or a new pickup truck without driving it? The third guest was probably the only honest one—"I just got married, so I can't come!"

As startling as the guests' excuses were, the response of the master of the household was even more unbelievable.

The servant came back and reported this to his master. Then the owner of the house became angry and ordered his servant, "Go out quickly into the streets and alleys of the town and bring in the poor, the crippled, the blind and the lame."

"Sir," the servant said, "what you ordered has been done, but there is still room."

Then the master told his servant, "Go out to the roads and country lanes and make them come in, so that my house will be full. I tell you, not one of those men who were invited will get a taste of my banquet." (Luke 14:21-24)

The servant was sent to a new group of people, people who never dreamed they would get an invitation to a banquet in such a classy neighborhood. The poor and crippled of the community had heard about the rich man, of course, but had no idea that he would ever extend an invitation to them. The people passing by the area on the roads didn't even know the rich man's name, but when they heard the invitation and saw the lavish feast already prepared, they eagerly joined in. They were so thrilled to be in the banquet hall that it didn't matter where they sat.

Jesus told that story to rebuke the proud religious people of his generation who were convinced that they had places of honor already reserved for them in God's kingdom. When the final invitation into kingdom life was issued, however, they refused to come. When the Jewish religious leaders heard Jesus' call to enter God's kingdom by believing in him as Savior and Lord, they began to make excuses. Most of the proud religious people of Israel rejected Jesus as God's promised Messiah. So God sent his servant out to the people in Israel who felt excluded from God's presence—the spiritually crippled and weak and blind—and they responded joyfully. Jesus attracted most of his followers from that part of the Jewish population who felt unworthy of God's attention. The leaders of the synagogues and the priests in the temple in Jerusalem may look down their pious noses at such people, but God in his grace welcomed them in.

Then God did something absolutely scandalous! He decided to invite people into his kingdom who had never even heard of him. God's invitation to the banquet feast of heaven went out to the Gentiles, the non-Jewish people of the world. In the Old Testament the door of salvation led through Israel. After Jesus' death and resurrection, the way was open to everyone. All a person had to do was respond in faith to God's gracious invitation. That's how all of us got into the banquet hall of God's love. We had no engraved invitation or elegant clothes. We just had our beggar's rags and the promise of the servant that whoever showed up at God's door in faith would be welcomed in.

Living Now in Light of the Not Yet

What impresses me most about this story is Jesus' description of the kingdom of God as a great banquet. It's an image the Bible uses often to paint a picture of the future kingdom of God on earth and the extension of that kingdom into eternity. Jesus said that many would come from every direction and would sit down with Abraham, Isaac and Jacob "in the kingdom of heaven" (Matthew 8:11; Luke 13:29). The kingdom is pictured as a wedding reception in which Jesus and his bride celebrate their union forever

(Matthew 25:10; Revelation 19:9). As he gave wine to his disciples just hours before his arrest and death, Jesus told them that he would not drink wine again until he drank it with his followers "in my Father's kingdom" (Matthew 26:29).

> "Let us celebrate, let us rejoice,
> let us give him glory!
> The marriage of the Lamb has come."
> —REVELATION 19:7 The Message

But this kingdom banquet will not be a stuffy, formal affair. Think again about the story Jesus told. Imagine how the mood of the banquet changed when the invited guests refused to come and all the street people showed up! They didn't know which fork to use first or how to operate the pepper mill, but they did know how to enjoy the bounty of the feast. The people in the chamber music ensemble loosened their ties and cranked out a little country-western music! Hugs, loud talk, clinking glassware and noisy kids were all part of the scene. The surprised participants couldn't believe how fortunate they were to be the guests of such a gracious, giving, rich man.

One of the joys of heaven will be the opportunity for limitless fellowship. We will sit with Jesus, with all the believers of the Old Testament, with the multitudes of Christians—and we will have no deadlines to meet. We won't feel rushed. We won't get tired.

Best of all, we will be totally unthreatened, so we will be able to focus all our attention on others, not on ourselves.

Since heaven is going to be such a celebration, maybe we should work at bringing a little more spontaneous joy into our gatherings with other Christians right now. There's certainly a time for seriousness and quiet reflection, but some of us have taken it too far. We've virtually banished joy from our lives and our relationships. We've practiced crabbiness so long that we've forgotten how to enjoy the bountiful goodness of God. You might start a real revolution at your church or in your small group or at the next fellowship dinner if you just smile—or laugh out loud!

One of the least recognized and appreciated aspects of God's character is his joy. We serve a joy-filled God! I am convinced that when we are ushered into the great banquet we call the kingdom of God, we will immediately know where Jesus is. We will hear his voice ringing with laughter.

Looking for a City

*"The talk they had with the Shining Ones was about the glory
of the place; who told them that the beauty and glory of it was inexpressible.
There, said they, is the Mount Zion, the heavenly Jerusalem,
the innumerable company of angels, and the spirits of just men made perfect.
You are going now, said they, to the paradise of God,
wherein you shall see the tree of life, and eat of the never-fading fruit thereof;
and when you come there, you shall have white robes given to you,
and your walk and talk shall be every day with the King,
even all the days of eternity."*

JOHN BUNYAN

A *s I write this, our granddaughter,* Allison, is just two months old. Her world consists of her mother's arms, her father's face, her blue-plaid infant seat and her crib. Once in a while she takes an excursion in the car to church or to the store, but she misses most of the trip by falling asleep. At other times she has to put up with the intrusion of other people who pass her around and talk to her in flutey little voices, trying to make her smile. Allison doesn't know yet about the wonders of a backyard swing set or picture books or the Internet or space travel. She is not equipped emotionally or physically or mentally to explore all the opportunities this world has to offer. I could sit down with Allison tomorrow for a few hours and start telling her about all the things she will eventually be able to investigate and enjoy, but I don't think much of it would sink in.

We face the same obstacle when it comes to comprehending the beauty and wonder and limitless possibilities of heaven. We aren't equipped to handle it yet! We aren't ready physically or emotionally or even spiritually to begin to envision and understand what an eternity in heaven will be like. We are as unprepared for heaven's glories as Allison is for the wonderful things all around her on earth.

Fortunately God saw our difficulty ahead of time. He tells us about heaven in images and words that we can at least begin to understand, but we have to realize that we aren't equipped to handle the full story yet. Someday we will be—and heaven will be far more magnificent and interesting and awesome than anything we can even imagine today. So as we look at the Bible's description of the new heaven and the new earth where we will live with the Lord forever, feel free to be dazzled—but remember that the ultimate reality will be a lot better.

Everything New
As wonderful as it will be to go to heaven at death or in the rap-

ture, that present dwelling place of God's people is only temporary. After Jesus reigns over the earth for a thousand years and after God's final judgment on those who have rejected his grace, God will do a marvelous new work of power. We will have grandstand seats for a new creation.

The problem with our present universe is that it is clothed in a shroud of sin. Adam's disobedience to God affected everything, not just human beings. The ground God created to produce an abundant supply of food began to require human toil and sweat before it would yield a harvest (Genesis 3:17-19). The apostle Paul saw the whole creation "groaning as in the pains of childbirth right up to the present time" (Romans 8:22).

The earth we live on and the universe around it are in the process of passing away. Someday God's first creation will come to an end, not because human beings destroy it and not because the sun burns out and life can't survive on earth any longer, but because God will sweep this creation away. The apostle Peter tells us exactly what will happen.

> The present heavens and earth by His word are being reserved for fire. . . . But the day of the Lord will come like a thief, in which the heavens will pass away with a roar and the elements will be destroyed with intense heat, and the earth and its works will be burned up. . . . The heavens will be destroyed by burning, and the elements will melt with intense heat! (2 Peter 3:7, 10, 12 NASB)

Peter is describing the total destruction of the earth and the planetary heavens that surround it. When Christ has reclaimed his creation that we have corrupted by sin and when he has conquered every enemy, this present universe will evaporate with a thunderous roar. The energy bound up in the atomic structure of the elements will be released, and the old creation will melt away.

When the old world is gone, God will step in and create a new dwelling place for his people. "But in keeping with [God's] promise we are looking forward to a new heaven and a new earth, the home of righteousness" (2 Peter 3:13).

In the apostle John's vision of heaven in the book of Revelation, he saw four new things in our eternal home. First, he saw a new heaven (Revelation 21:1), a newly created universe. The word translated "new" in our English Bible is the Greek work *kainos*, which means "newly made." God will not just patch up the old universe. With his awesome power he will fashion a new universe before our eyes.

John also saw a new earth, "for the first heaven and the first earth had passed away, and there was no longer any sea" (Revelation 21:1). Is this new earth like our present earth? Probably not. There is no ocean on the new earth, no blockades of water that divide people from each other. Later in his vision John sees an enormous city resting on the new earth—a city that would throw our present spinning earth out of orbit and into the sun! God's new earth probably won't rotate, since John says that there is no night there (21:25). The new universe may have a sun and a moon, but they won't be needed to light the earth since the radiance of God lights it continuously (21:23; 22:5). An old hymn says that "time will be no more" in heaven, but the Bible indicates that we will mark the passage of time in heaven. John is told that the tree of life that flourishes in heaven will bear "twelve crops of fruit, yielding its fruit every *month*" (22:2, emphasis added).

Third, John saw that *everything* in the future creation will be new. "He who was seated on the throne said, 'I am making everything new!' " (Revelation 21:5). The eternal phase of heaven will be so unlike what we are familiar with that our present language can't even describe it.

Some things will be missing in the new creation, but they won't be missed. The curse that rests on the old order of things won't apply to the new creation (Revelation 22:3). Death, mourning, suffering and pain will be no more, and God "will wipe every tear from [our] eyes" (21:4). Those whose names are written in the Lamb's book of life "will see his face, and his name will be on their foreheads" (22:4). No evil will lure us away from pure devotion to Christ. Satan, our enemy and tempter, will be confined in the lake of fire forever (20:10).

The Holy City
The fourth "new" aspect that John saw in his vision of heaven was a magnificent city.

I saw the Holy City, the new Jerusalem, coming down out of heaven from God, prepared as a bride beautifully dressed for her husband. And I heard a loud voice from the throne saying, "Now the dwelling of God is with men, and he will live with them. They will be his people, and God himself will be with them and be their God." (Revelation 21:2-3)

John describes our future home as a city with walls and gates and streets and rivers, with buildings and people. The new Jerusalem will be a city without flaw, dazzling in its brilliance and beauty, a city whose architect and builder is God (Hebrews 11:10). It is a *holy* city, uninfected by evil and reserved for God's holy people. The city is the eternal tabernacle, the dwelling of God and his people forever. You will never be a refugee from heaven.

John tries to describe the city in terms of the most precious jewels and costliest metals known. The gates are massive single pearls, the foundations are enormous jewels, the streets are pure gold, polished like glass (Revelation 21:18-21).

"What do we count most valuable on earth?
Gold. Men live for gold, kill for it.
But in heaven gold is so plentiful
that they pave the streets with it." —F. B. Meyer

The angel who escorted John on his tour of heaven measured the city. Its width and length and height are equal, making a cube (or pyramid) that measures fourteen hundred miles in each direction. That is roughly the distance from the Mississippi River to the Atlantic Ocean, from the U.S.-Canada border to the Gulf of Mexico and from the earth's surface one-twentieth of the way to our moon—the size of a small planet! Someone has calculated that a building that high would have 780,000 floors in it. No shortage of rooms in that apartment complex! John doesn't say if the city rests on the new earth or if it's suspended above the new earth or if the city *is* the new earth. It is challenging enough for him simply to try to describe this magnificent eternal home of ours.

John doesn't mention seeing a hospital in the new city since there is no more sickness or pain. Physical defects and disabilities will be gone forever. The only person carrying scars into heaven will be Jesus. Even in his resurrection body, the nail scars in his hands and feet and the wound in his side were still visible as reminders of what he suffered for our salvation (John 20:27). John doesn't mention a cemetery in heaven either, because there is no more death. No prisons will be needed—or police stations. Another thing John doesn't mention is a church building. The Christians who spend their time debating the minor points of denominational differences and arguing over worship styles might be surprised at the absence of churches, temples and altars. In this holy city the Lord God Almighty and the Lamb are the temple. Denominational walls will have crumbled, bringing us all together to focus our spiritual activity and worship, not on a service or a building or a system of doctrine but totally on the Father and the Son.

We will meet millions of people in heaven too. The city has twelve gates, not one—three gates on each side, so people will enter the city from all directions (Revelation 21:12-13). They will come from all parts of the world, from every level of society, from every direction on the theological compass and from every generation since time began. But we will all be bound together by our faith and devotion to the Lord Jesus Christ.

Whenever I talk about heaven, someone asks if we will know each other in eternity. I think we will—and on a much deeper level than we know each other now. Jesus was recognized by his disciples after his resurrection. When Jesus took Peter, James and John up a mountain and was transfigured before them, the three disciples recognized Moses and Elijah, who came to converse with Jesus (Matthew 17:2-4). How did they recognize men who had lived hundreds of years earlier? I think the disciples had a taste of the intuitive knowledge we will have in eternity.

"As John watches, an entire city, magnificent in its glory,
descends whole from heaven and becomes part of the new earth.
Heaven and earth are now one. The heavenly realm
has moved its capital city intact to a new earth."—JOHN MACARTHUR

I am also persuaded that we will know people as we have

known them on earth. I will know my parents as my parents and my children as my children. Even though Jesus made it clear that we will not reproduce in heaven (Matthew 22:30), I think I will know that Karen was my wife on earth. What I'm convinced we *won't* know is who is missing in heaven. Those friends and family members who reject Christ and are condemned will be erased from our memories—along with any memory of our sins and failures and disobedience here on earth. Heaven would not be an experience without tears or pain if we had to live with regret over our past or with remorse for those separated from us.

Eternity Is a Long Time

If most of us were honest about how we feel about eternity in heaven, we would have to admit that while heaven sounds like a spectacular place, eternity is a long time. Won't we get bored? Actually, heaven will be a place of complete fulfillment and challenging activity and limitless opportunities. The Bible only gives us snapshots of our involvement, but we certainly won't be bored. I find at least five activities that will occupy our minds and hearts and bodies for eternity.

First, as we've already seen, we will enjoy *worship without distraction*.[1] Heavenly worship will not be confining or manipulated but spontaneous and genuine. We will express our praise and adoration to God without the distraction of time, without the discomfort of physical fatigue and without inhibition. We will lose ourselves in the sheer joy of expressing with our lips the love we feel for God in our hearts. As you read the book of Revelation, you won't find much preaching in heaven. That bothers those of us who are preachers, but it's a fact. What you *will* find is uninterrupted praise and worship. We will stand, kneel and fall on our faces— and we won't care what those around us think. All we will care about is that God knows how much we love him.

A second area of involvement in heaven will be *service without exhaustion*. John wrote, "[God's] servants will serve him" (Revelation 22:3). Eight times in the book of Revelation the word *serve* is used to describe our activity in heaven. Maybe that service will be a continuation and expansion of the ministry we have on earth. Whatever it is, we will be able to serve without frustration or the fear of failure or the exhaustion that so limits our ministries here on earth.

One part of our service in heaven will be to reign with Christ. Paul told us that we will someday judge the world and even judge angels (1 Corinthians 6:2-3). Paul promised Timothy that those who endure faithfully will reign with Christ (2 Timothy 2:12). Even in the eternal phase of heaven "we will reign for ever and ever" (Revelation 22:5). Exactly what form that authority and responsibility will take is not spelled out, but it will be suited perfectly to our abilities and will reflect our faithfulness in the work God gives us to do today.

Fellowship without fear will also occupy us in eternity. We will enjoy the company of thousands of angels, an incredible gathering of Christians, millions of Old Testament believers and Jesus himself (Hebrews 12:22-23). We will have time to relax around the table with Abraham, Isaac and Jacob along with Daniel and Paul and Ruth and Elijah (Matthew 8:11) —and we will have a lot to talk about. We will be able to focus all our attention and energy on others instead of on ourselves.

I always enjoy watching my wife, Karen, at a fellowship dinner or banquet at our church. She's usually the last one to eat the meal because she is walking around, talking to people and meeting visitors. She tries to get to every table and speak to every person. I'm dashing for the food line while she is seeing to it that everyone has a seat and knows the people around them. I have a feeling that our time around the banquet table in heaven will not be focused on the food but simply on the joy of being together.

Heaven will also be an opportunity to learn. We sometimes think that we will know all there is to know when we are glorified, but that is not the case. Instead God will give us an infinite capacity to learn. The wonder of *learning without fatigue* will be another of the joys of heaven. Not only will we learn from each other, but we will also be given more and more truth from God. Paul said that in the coming ages God will take us deeper and deeper into a knowledge of "the incomparable riches of his grace" (Ephesians 2:7). Heaven will give us the privilege of unraveling the greatest mysteries of God's grace to us.

I think heaven will also extend to us the opportunity to fulfill all the potential God gave us as human beings. I have always loved the cello, but I've never taken the time (or effort) to learn how to play it. Perhaps in the ages of eternity I will be able to learn to play the cello and use its tones to express praise and adoration to God. Think about all the possibilities that you have wanted to explore in this life—mountain climbing or painting or singing tenor in the choir. Then think about having an endless amount of time and boundless energy and the potential to use fully the creativity God deposited within you.

The final activity and blessing of heaven will be *rest without boredom* from our difficult labors on earth (Revelation 14:13). Our rest will not be rest from weariness; resurrected bodies don't get tired! It will be a rest from want, the empowering rest found in God's presence alone. In heaven we will be perfectly content and satisfied forever.

Living Now in Light of the Not Yet

When we think about heaven, we sometimes forget that we have the potential to live a heavenly life right now. In Ephesians 2:6 Paul says that we are already seated in the heavenly realms in Christ Jesus. We are heirs of all of God's riches, and we have the down payment on our full inheritance in the Holy Spirit who lives within us (Ephesians 1:13-14). We have the blessings of fellowship with God right now. All the activities that will occupy us in eternity can fill our lives every day. Eternal life doesn't start when we die; it started the moment we believed in Christ. We possess a whole new kind of life in him!

A lot of Christians look at heaven and think it will be boring because their Christian lives here are boring. But if your relationship with Christ is uneventful and unexciting and unfulfilling, it's because you haven't laid claim to the resources that God has already promised and provided. We have the Word of God to lead us and encourage us—but we don't spend much time in it. We have the power of God's Spirit resident within us—but we aren't cultivating any relationship with the Spirit. We have other believers to stimulate us to consistent, faithful living—but we don't even get involved in other people's lives.

Every day provides fresh opportunities to invest in eternal things. What amazes me is how God uses our smallest efforts to produce abundant results. My father pastored a church near Detroit in the late 1950s. Several decades later my parents were invited back to that church for an anniversary celebration. A man came up to my father and said, "You don't know me, but I know you. When you were the pastor here, you made a hospital visit one day to a man from your church. I was in the bed next to that man. As you read Scripture and prayed with him, the Lord convicted me about my own separation from God. Shortly after that, I trusted Christ as my Savior and Lord." The man was still actively involved in the ministry and outreach of that church.

Christians are sometimes accused of being so heavenly minded that we aren't of much earthly good. I don't think that is the problem. The Bible challenges us to set our hearts and minds on things above, not on earthly things (Colossians 3:1-2). God hasn't told us about heaven's glories so that we will dress in white robes and sit on a mountaintop waiting for Jesus to come. He has told us what lies ahead so we will think more seriously about our responsibility to serve Christ with a whole heart. God has told us about heaven so we will live courageous lives here and now. We know how God's story ends, and we have nothing to fear from the world around us. That confident assurance of heaven gives us the strength to walk into the fire of persecution—or the workplace where God has put us. The apostle Peter put it this way:

> Since everything will be destroyed in this way, what kind of people ought you to be? You ought to live holy and godly lives as you look forward to the day of God and speed its coming. . . . So then, dear friends, since you are looking forward to this, make every effort to be found spotless, blameless and at peace with him. (2 Peter 3:11-12, 14)

Notes

Chapter 1: Preparing a Place

[1]The New International Version of the Bible uses the word *sky* to refer to the atmospheric and cosmic heavens. In the New American Standard Bible translation of Genesis 1:20, for example, birds fly across "the expanse of the *heavens.*" In the NIV, birds fly across "the expanse of the *sky.*"

[2]"Heaven," in *Dictionary of Biblical Imagery,* ed. Leland Ryken, James C. Wilhoit and Tremper Longman III (Downers Grove, Ill.: InterVarsity Press, 1998), p. 372.

[3]To learn more about what the Bible teaches about angels, see Douglas Connelly, *Angels Around Us* (Downers Grove, Ill.: InterVarsity Press, 1983).

[4]1994 Gallup Poll, published in *The Detroit Free Press*, April 6, 1997.

Chapter 2: The Final Frontier

[1]This account is told in George Guthrie, *Hebrews: The NIV Application Commentary* (Grand Rapids, Mich.: Zondervan, 1998), p. 121.

Chapter 5: Thy Kingdom Come

[1]The Old Testament prophetic books are filled with references to the glory of God's kingdom. Some of the key texts are Psalm 2:6-12; 72:8-11; Isaiah 2:4; 4:2-6; 9:7; 11:1-12; 32:1-5; 35:1-10; 65:20-25; Jeremiah 31:3-9; 33:14-16; 34:23-24; Ezekiel 40—48; Daniel 2:31-45; 7:14; Hosea 3:4-5; Joel 2:28-32; Amos 9:11-15; Micah 4:1-8; Zechariah 9:9-10; 12:8-10.

Chapter 10: Looking for a City

[1]I'm indebted to Don Baker for these categories. See Don Baker, *Heaven* (Portland, Ore.: Multnomah Press, 1983).